MARK

A Devotional Commentary

MARK
A Devotional Commentary

Meditations on the Gospel According to St. Mark

GENERAL EDITOR
Leo Zanchettin

The Word Among Us
9639 Doctor Perry Road
Ijamsville, Maryland 21754
www.wau.org
ISBN: 0-932085-13-X

Scripture quotations are from the Revised Standard Version of the
Bible, copyright 1946, 1952, 1971, by the Division of Christian
Education of the National Council of the Churches of Christ in the
U.S.A. Used by permission.

Cover art: Erich Lessing/Art Resource, NY
Vivarini, Bartolomeo. Triptych of Saint Mark
Cover design by David Crosson
Copy Editor: Laura Worsham

Made and printed in the United States of America.

Foreword

Dear Friends in Christ:

Just as he was about to invite a rich young man to become one of his disciples, Jesus looked upon him with great love (see Mark 10:21). It was a moment of tenderness and compassion, a moment when Jesus offered the young man a glimpse into the love that could change his whole life if he would only embrace it.

It is this look of love that Jesus invites all of us to experience whenever we read this gospel. Through the writings of people like St. Mark, we can encounter Jesus and be transformed by him. Whether we are reading about his miracles, his teachings to his followers, or his death and resurrection, our hearts can be moved by Jesus' love for us and our minds can be filled with the truth of his gospel.

These are the goals we had in mind when we set out to produce this devotional commentary on the Gospel of Mark. In the chapters that follow, you will find short commentaries that explain the various passages in Mark and give words of encouragement to help you experience Jesus' love. As you pray through this gospel, may the Holy Spirit open your heart to the wonders of knowing Jesus in this way.

We want to thank everyone who has made this commentary possible. Many of the meditations produced here were initially developed for *The Word Among Us* monthly publication, and we want to thank all of the writers of these meditations for granting us permission to reprint their work. In addition, we want to thank Fr. Joseph Mindling, O.F.M. Cap., and Gregory Roa for their contributions. In a special way, we thank Patricia Mitchell, without whose contributions and editorial skills this book would not have been possible. May the Lord abundantly bless each of them for their service.

Finally, we want to ask the Holy Spirit expand our vision of Jesus. May he reveal to us more and more deeply the love, power, and glory of the Son of God and Messiah.

Leo Zanchettin
General Editor

Table of Contents

An Introduction to Mark's Gospel

By Fr. Joseph A. Mindling, O.F.M. Cap.

The Gospel according to Mark is printed in every Christian Bible, but, even so, it has managed to remain (in many ways) like the pearl of great price buried in a field, waiting to be discovered and able to enrich spiritual treasure seekers with unexpected rewards. Those who would harvest this fortune must approach it with awareness, prayer, and determination.

Christians in the first century already esteemed Mark's Gospel, which proclaims itself in its opening line as "The Good News of Jesus Christ" (Mark 1:1). More like a pamphlet than a book, it set a pattern for the way in which many would tell the story of Jesus' life. Succeeding generations continued to copy it carefully in order to make its message available to the ever-expanding number of those who (like the Roman Centurion in 15:39) recognized that Jesus truly was the Son of God. Compared to the other three gospels, however, Mark received much less exposure in the public liturgical prayer of the church for many centuries. Writers during the whole first millennium were much slower to produce commentaries on Mark like those that were being prepared on Matthew, Luke, and John.

In fact, it was only during relatively recent times that modern readers and scholars have rediscovered this shortest, and probably oldest, narrative in the New Testament. Given the eager interest in the Gospel of Mark today (e.g., its important place in the

Lectionary and in many recent books and articles), its low profile in the past may strike us as somewhat puzzling.

This delayed popular reaction was certainly not based on doubts about the apostolic foundations of Mark's account. Fathers of the Church like Irenaeus, Tertullian, and Clement of Alexandria all handed on the tradition that the author was the same John Mark who had served with the missionaries Paul and Barnabas and who later worked with Peter in Rome. Most modern experts still agree that what we sometimes call "the second gospel" (because it stands between Matthew and Luke in modern Bibles) was completed and starting to circulate among communities of believers within thirty to forty years after Jesus' ascension from the dead.

Its first readers lived in turbulent times. The Good News was spreading quickly, but the apostolic generation was growing older and encountering violent persecution, even as it was seeing numerous conversions. Both outside and inside the church, curiosity and excitement were high, but so were distortions and rumors about who Jesus really was. Individuals who had developed a positive attitude toward him, and even those who had recently embraced Christianity, needed to deepen and strengthen their new religious bearings. The Gospel of Mark addressed these needs in poignant but unpretentious prose that first-time readers still find quite engaging today.

All through history, those who are called by the Father to unite themselves with his Son must examine and re-examine Jesus' identity. Who is Jesus for all of us; who is Jesus for me? Somehow, our response to these questions and the growth of our life in Christ are linked together. One of the special characteristics of the second gospel is the way it describes the insistent but gradual way in which Jesus revealed himself to his followers—the struggle they went through to grasp and accept what he was preparing them to understand. As we read and pray about the Gospel of Mark, it is often possible to identify with the episodes described. We can take consolation in the fact that faith and understanding have always been hard-won prizes, even for those who enjoyed the visible presence of the Lord.

The Gospels of Matthew, Luke, and John record more of the spoken words of Jesus, including practical instruction about living out our faith commitment after we have received his call to new life. Without these longer teachings, our attention is naturally drawn more in the Gospel of Mark to the actions of Jesus. We see his power dominating the forces of evil and sickness, but we also see the strength of will that enables our Lord to accomplish the mission preordained for him by his Heavenly Father.

Our modern translations of the Marcan gospel are divided into sixteen chapters. In the first half of these accounts, Jesus moves through a life of public teaching and service, marked by the performance of many prodigious signs. He calms a storm at sea and walks upon the waves. He feeds two huge groups of hungry people. He cures many—a man with a withered hand, a woman with recurrent bleeding, a blind beggar, a paralytic. He relieves Peter's mother-in-law of a fever and heals a deaf man with a speech impediment. At times, great crowds bring their sick to Jesus and he cures them immediately. He even brings a little girl back to life.

As we observe and listen to Jesus through Mark's words, we are reminded that what the first disciples learned about their Master involved some challenging truths. Paradoxically, they also needed to unlearn some presuppositions that they had already formed. After witnessing all these things, when Jesus asks the disciples who they think that he is, Peter responds: "You are the Christ" (Mark 8:29). Since the prophet Isaiah had spoken about a "Servant of the Lord" who would work wonders for the people, a group of observant

Jewish men could well begin to wonder if someone like Jesus was the fulfillment of such predictions. Why couldn't he be the long-awaited "Christ," the heir apparent to the royal house of Judah? What startles us is that Jesus immediately warns the apostles not to tell anyone about him!

His followers had arrived at the correct "title"—the anointed descendant of King David. But Jesus knew that they were not ready to share their primary conclusions about him. They still needed to grasp other truths that would set in proper context any incomplete or incorrect images of the Messiah they had already formed. The missing element that they needed to learn was the mystery of the cross. Three separate times after the high point of Peter's declaration, Jesus insisted that his future will be more tragic and more wonderful than they could imagine:

> The Son of Man must suffer many things, and be rejected by the elders and the chief priests and the scribes, and be killed, and after three days rise again. (Mark 8:31; see also 9:31, 10:33-34)

Anyone who was personally involved with the Messiah could not remain simply a passive observer. To share in the mission of the Son of Man is to share in his destiny. When Peter tried to take issue with Jesus' prediction of his own fate, the Master summoned the crowd with his disciples and said to them:

> If any man would come after me, let him deny himself and take up his cross and follow me. For whoever would save his life will lose it; and whoever loses his life for my sake and the gospel's will save it. For what does it profit a man, to gain the whole world and forfeit his life? (Mark 8:34-36)

This is the heart of what has been dubbed "the Marcan paradox." As we are able to enter into the experience of the first followers of Christ (through the gospel narrative and our prayerful union with it), we watch the evidence mount. Jesus has power over life and death; Jesus can forgive sinners; Jesus is the Son of man who will return upon the clouds as cosmic judge. It is easy to understand the bewilderment of the disciples when this glorious picture was joined with a forecast of betrayal by the highest religious authorities and a brutal murder by crucifixion.

Deepening the enigma even more, Mark pointed to the mysterious encounter of the divine and the human in the person of the Galilean Rabbi. He reports the awe-inspiring revelations that took place at Jesus' baptism and at the transfiguration (Mark 1:11, 9:7), his post-resurrection appearances to witnesses who could hardly believe their eyes and ears, and his glorious ascension into heaven (16:1-20). We also learn of episodes where even the diabolical opponents of Jesus blurt out acknowledgments of his special relationship with the Most High God (1:24, 5:7).

With an eye for details not always recorded by the other gospels, Mark shows fascinating aspects of the human side of the Messiah as well: That Jesus liked to eat with his friends, that he used a little pillow to sleep on in the boat, that he hugged little children and enjoyed being with them, that he did not always hide strong emotions, that he used mud in the performance of a miracle, that he listened carefully to the parents of a little girl who had died, and that he was fearful before he himself died. Individually, many of these observations may not catch our attention, but collectively they deepen our understanding of what it meant for the Son of God to take on our human nature and share our everyday life.

The book you hold in your hands is a helpful companion for the modern reader of the Gospel according to Mark. Although its pages are tempered by solid Biblical scholarship, this commentary

is not designed to supply anyone with a new dimension of archae-
ological or historical data. Rather, it is an invitation to join with
the chosen band of Jesus' followers, to walk among them, to listen, to talk to, and to be with the Master. Like the disciples, we
can expand our religious vision beyond the limits of our earlier
horizons.

Perhaps the larger history of Christianity's reaction to this
particular gospel has some wisdom to offer us about the way we
may best approach it on an individual level. One major reason
that modern writers offer for why interest in Mark was slow to
develop during the early centuries is that many simply presumed
they already knew its "story line" from having read the other
gospels—especially Matthew and Luke. Like children, it is always
more likely that we will miss the most important and interesting
parts of high-quality literature when we think we know the plot.
In truth, that is often the point at which in-depth understanding
really begins!

A new spiritual experience with this gospel usually requires
three conditions. First, we need to come to it humbly, acknowledging that there is still much we need to know. We start out with
what our faith has taught us about what Jesus means for everyone.
But this is incomplete until we understand why each of us needs
the Messiah now. Second, we must come to the inspired text with
the trust that God will continue to use it as a place where we can
encounter Jesus as his first followers did. Third, we need the grace
to see the gospel as a vehicle of prayer. On this foundation, our
careful reading about what Jesus did and how he suffered for us
can move beyond being simply *about* him into reflections under-
taken *with him*.

We read most books to be entertained or educated. The Gospel
of Mark was written to change our minds as well as our hearts—if
we have the courage to open them to its hidden treasures. It is not

just a "good read"; it is an opportunity for discovery. As we bring to it our desire to know more about Jesus and more about ourselves, we can claim for our own the words of the opening prayer from the feast of Mark the Evangelist:

> Father, you gave St. Mark the privilege of proclaiming your gospel. May we profit by his wisdom and follow Christ more faithfully.

Scripture: The Language of God

By Patricia Mitchell

Sacred Scripture is the speech of God as it is put down in writing under the breath of the Holy Spirit. (Vatican II: Dei Verbum 9)

What is it about the Bible that has held the love and fascination of so many men and women over the ages? As the Vatican II Council declared, scripture is the voice of God speaking to us in our own human language. The Bible is an ocean in which we can immerse ourselves and never fully discover its riches. God's very life flows through it. As a nurse pricks a vein to draw blood, we can tap into this power for ourselves by faithfully praying with the scriptures each day.

The Bible is really a collection of many books, written by different authors over a long span of time. The Vatican II document, the *Dogmatic Constitution on Divine Revelation* or *Dei Verbum*, noted that God inspired the human authors of the sacred books, acting "in them and by them" (*Dei Verbum*, 11). It was "as true authors that they consigned to writing whatever he wanted written, and no more" (*Dei Verbum*, 11). Although God used a variety of authors to put down his word, as St. Augustine wrote, "it is one and the same Utterance that resounds in the mouths of all the sacred writers."

The Bible is also a story, and we are part of the script. The story begins at the dawn of creation, when God, out of pure love, created the universe and mankind to live in harmony with him. But man rejected God's plan, and our paradise was lost. Then throughout the Old Testament, we see the Father reaching out to his people, calling them back to him.

Finally, the Father sends his Son to rescue us; Jesus becomes flesh. In the gospels, we meet God with a human face, whose words and actions cut to the heart. Even after Jesus dies for us and rises from the dead, the story is not over. He sends his Holy Spirit so that we, his disciples, can build his kingdom on earth. Someday, we will live in glory with the Trinity in the new heaven and new earth.

For now, we are like the disciples on the road to Emmaus (Luke 24:13-35). Jesus himself can draw near to us, as he did to those on the road, and "open to us the scriptures" (24:32). Through his Holy Spirit, our hearts can "burn within us" (24:32). We can make better progress on our journey through the scriptures if we adopt certain attitudes and habits to help us along the way.

Most importantly, we must expect, in faith, that God will reveal himself to us through scripture. If we have doubts, we can ask God to show us his face through the words we read. If we need a message of encouragement or hope, we can ask the Holy Spirit to lead us to the right passage. Often, the Lord will help us to discern his will for us through a particular scripture, as he has for so many Christians who have gone before us. We can trust that God will show us the way through his word.

We also can consciously affirm our belief in what we read. There have been attempts over the years to "explain away" the miracles in the Bible and to view the resurrection as a figurative rather than a literal event. This dissipates not only the power of scripture, but also the reality that the Lord can act in our lives in the same way. In John's Gospel, just before Jesus raised Lazarus, he said to Martha: "I am the resurrection and the life . . . . Do you believe this?" (John 11:25-26). Jesus asks us the same question. We can respond as Martha did: "Yes Lord; I believe" (11:27).

The Mind of Christ

Scripture will impact us if we are open to being changed by what we read. The Lord cannot work with prideful, hard-hearted people who are unwilling to budge from their own view of things. God's ways and thoughts are above ours (Isaiah 55:9). If we want "the mind of Christ" (1 Corinthians 2:16), we need to come to the Lord and ask him to transform us.

According to St. Paul, scripture can form us and help us to lead holy lives: "All scripture is inspired by God and profitable for teaching, for reproof, for correction, and for training in righteousness" (2 Timothy 3:16-17). Coupled with the teachings of the Church, scripture is our objective moral compass, helping us to see where we have strayed and giving us the humility and courage to repent and receive God's mercy.

Praying the Word

It is crucial that we spend time every day searching the scriptures and using them to pray. The Bible is one book that we should never put aside. As we come to daily prayer, we can open to the scriptures to see if God wants to speak to us through them. The second Vatican Council said that prayer "should accompany the reading of sacred Scripture, so that a dialogue takes place between God and man" (*Dei Verbum*, 25). We can read passages we have read many times before, and still discover a new insight or truth. Unlike most books, the scriptures never get old. As in a bottomless treasure chest, we can always find new rewards.

Praying with the words of scripture is a time-honored way of drawing closer to the Lord. The Bible is full of phrases that can dispose us to receiving God's love and mercy. When we are asking God for forgiveness, we can pray the words of the blind beggar:

"Jesus, Son of David, have mercy on me" (Mark 10:47). When we are trying to accept a difficult situation in our lives, we can pray with Jesus in the Garden of Gethsemane: "Father, if you are willing, remove this cup from me; nevertheless not my will, but yours, be done" (Luke: 22:42). When we are struggling to forgive someone who has hurt us, we can pray: "Father, forgive them; for they know not what they do" (Luke 23:34).

The psalms, too, are full of words of praise, of thanksgiving, of joy, of contrition, and even of complaint. For every emotion we may experience, there is a prayer we can pray from scripture, one that has been repeated countless times by believers throughout the centuries.

Making the effort to learn more about the history and culture of people and places in the Old and New Testaments can reap its own rewards. Passages that can be difficult to interpret come alive when we better understand the context in which they were written and what the authors had in mind as they wrote. Through study, we can also better understand how the Old Testament was fulfilled in the New.

As we immerse ourselves in scripture, we become "fluent" in the language of the Bible, and the Lord can speak to us even when we are not reading it. When we have a working knowledge and love for his word, he can bring it to our minds and hearts in the daily circumstances of our lives. Because scripture is "alive," we experience the presence of God through his living word. For example, if we are feeling afraid, the Father may encourage us with the words of his Son: "Do not fear, only believe" (Mark 5:36). If we are exhausted, we may remember Jesus' words to come to him with our burdens, and we can rest in him (Matthew 11:28).

Best of all, when we fill our minds with scripture, we come to know Jesus as our true friend and brother. We can use our imagination and see ourselves as part of the crowd, hanging on to every word he uttered. We can recall how he wept when Lazarus died (John 11:35), and be confident that he weeps with us too over our sorrows. We can kneel by his side, washing the feet of the people he puts in our lives (John 13:3-11). We can be like Mary, anointing him with the precious perfume of our love (John 12:3). Every story in scripture, and especially in the gospels, was put there by God for a purpose. These stories span time and space—they are there for us to experience Jesus. He lives among us.

"In the sacred books, the Father who is in heaven comes lovingly to meet his children, and talks with them. And such is the force and power of the Word of God that it can serve the Church as her support and vigor, and the children of the Church as strength for their faith, food for the soul, and a pure and lasting fount of spiritual life" (*Dei Verbum*, 21). Let us come to the table of the Lord daily to sustain us on our journey to everlasting life.

The Prologue

MARK
1:1–15

Mark 1:1-8

¹ The beginning of the gospel of Jesus Christ, the Son of God. ² As it is written in Isaiah the prophet, "Behold, I send my messenger before thy face, who shall prepare thy way; ³ the voice of one crying in the wilderness: Prepare the way of the Lord, make his paths straight—" ⁴ John the baptizer appeared in the wilderness, preaching a baptism of repentance for the forgiveness of sins. ⁵ And there went out to him all the country of Judea, and all the people of Jerusalem; and they were baptized by him in the river Jordan, confessing their sins. ⁶ Now John was clothed with camel's hair, and had a leather girdle around his waist, and ate locusts and wild honey. ⁷ And he preached, saying, "After me comes he who is mightier than I, the thong of whose sandals I am not worthy to stoop down and untie. ⁸ I have baptized you with water; but he will baptize you with the Holy Spirit."

Believing Jews knew that one day the Messiah would come among them. The teachings of the prophets made it clear. Isaiah had spoken of a voice crying, "Prepare the way of the LORD. . . . Every valley shall be lifted up, and every mountain and hill be made low" (Isaiah 40:3,4). Malachi predicted a messenger preparing the way for "the Lord whom you seek" (Malachi 3:1). John the Baptist, the voice and the messenger, likewise prepared the way by preaching repentance for the forgiveness of sins (Mark 1:4).

Through a renewal of faith and life, we can prepare our hearts to welcome Jesus more deeply. This renewal is not something that can be satisfactorily completed by changing a few minor details of daily living. After all, lowering mountains, filling in valleys, and making rough ways smooth is not an easy task. God has in mind something even more radical—the coming of a new heaven and a new earth, a new kingdom where peace, forgiveness, reconciliation with God, and righteousness will reign, beginning even now (2 Peter 3:13).

We face a moment of decision. If we are to be participants with Jesus in ushering in this new heaven and new earth, we must heed John the Baptist's call to repentance and choose the new life Jesus came to bring. We need to look to Jesus, "the Lamb of God, who takes away the sin of the world" (John 1:29), and prepare to offer him the fruit of our repentance.

Perhaps you recognize the voice of the Holy Spirit speaking to you of sin in your life. We may need to remove mountains of unbelief, pride, and self-will or fill in valleys of despondency and feelings of inferiority. Perhaps we need to make untruthful and dishonest ways straight, and thus begin to remove barriers separating us from God and preventing the holiness he looks for in our lives (2 Peter 3:14).

Act on this grace. Take the time to make an examination of conscience, and then receive the Sacrament of Reconciliation. It is only as we renounce sin and accept forgiveness from God that we will know the transforming power of new life and experience the joy of a new heaven and a new earth.

"Lord Jesus, thank you for bringing us new life. Give us the grace to perceive the sinful patterns in our lives and the humility to repent of them. We want to follow you."

Mark 1:9-11

⁹ In those days Jesus came from Nazareth of Galilee and was baptized by John in the Jordan. ¹⁰ And when he came up out of the water, immediately he saw the heavens opened and the Spirit descending upon him like a dove; ¹¹ and a voice came from heaven, "Thou art my beloved Son; with thee I am well pleased."

At Jesus' baptism, the heavens were opened to him, and the mystery of the Trinity was made manifest. He heard his Father's voice bestowing his blessing on him, and the Spirit descended upon him like a dove. Jesus of Nazareth, the sinless one, identified himself with our fallen humanity by accepting a baptism of repentance. Because of his obedience to the Father's will for him, because of his willingness to embrace our sin and destroy it on the cross, Jesus showed himself to be the beloved, faithful Son of God. He showed himself to be the servant of the Lord whose death would result in the outpouring of the Spirit on us all.

Having been immersed in the life God had destined for him, Jesus went into the world proclaiming the kingdom of God and performing miracles. It was out of the abundance of this Spirit that Jesus was able to do the things that he did and to manifest God's love so completely. Now, he would prepare his people to receive the same Holy Spirit in whom he had been immersed.

We who have been baptized into Christ have received this Spirit. We too can hear the Father say of us, "This is my beloved." We can know and witness to the love and power of God active in our lives. Fr. Raniero Cantalamessa, preacher to the papal household, has commented on these truths, saying: "We have been saved so that we would be capable of doing in our turn, through grace and faith, the good works God had prepared beforehand for us which are the fruits of the Spirit" (*Mary Mirror of the Church*, p. 71). "The fire of the Spirit was given to us at Baptism. We must remove the ashes suffocating it so that it can be flame again and make us capable of loving" (*Life in the Lordship of Jesus Christ*, p. 154).

Let us re-examine our baptism in light of Jesus' baptism for us. We were baptized into Jesus' death. If we die with him, we also rise with him, forgiven and filled with divine life. Everything has been given to us in Christ! We must only continue, daily, to surrender to the Lord and look for the work of the Spirit in our lives.

Mark 1:12-15

[12] The Spirit immediately drove him out into the wilderness. [13] And he was in the wilderness forty days, tempted by Satan; and he was with the wild beasts; and the angels ministered to him. [14] Now after John was arrested, Jesus came into Galilee, preaching the gospel of God, [15] and saying, "The time is fulfilled, and the kingdom of God is at hand; repent, and believe in the gospel."

B efore the world began, God knew us, loved us, and called us to know and to love him. The Old Testament describes a number of covenants that God made with his people to prepare them to receive his life more fully. Time and again, however, God's people failed to uphold his covenants and, as a consequence, they separated themselves from his love and protection.

Yet God loved the world so much that in the fullness of time he sent his only begotten Son to teach, to heal, and ultimately to die, establishing a new, unending covenant in his blood. This is the new covenant that God promised through Ezekiel: "A new heart I will give you, and a new spirit I will put within you . . . . I will put my spirit within you, and cause you to walk in my statutes" (Ezekiel 36:26-27).

We enter into this new covenant at baptism and, by lives of faith, we allow the Spirit to unite us with Jesus more fully each day. We become a new creation in Christ. Having died with him, it is no longer we who live, but Christ who lives in us (see Galatians 2:20).

This miracle of baptism into a new covenant is prefigured in many ways in the Old Testament, but there is none more colorful than the story of Noah (Genesis 6-9). From its earliest days, the church has seen in the flood an image of the water of baptism, which washes away the sins of the flesh and gives humanity a new beginning.

Our new beginning in baptism is a participation in Jesus' life. Just as he was tested in the wilderness for forty days, we too will experience times of testing and growth. God gives us these seasons to teach us to surrender ourselves to him more fully and to show us how utterly faithful he is to his promises. He loves us so much that he will never abandon us. All he asks is that we trust him— just as Noah and his family did—to see us through the storms.

"Heavenly Father, speak your words of covenant love to us. By your Spirit, help us to trust more fully in you so that, like your Son, Jesus, we would be heralds of your kingdom on earth."

The Authority of the Son of God

MARK
1:16–3:35

Mark 1:16-20

[16] And passing along by the Sea of Galilee, he saw Simon and Andrew the brother of Simon casting a net in the sea; for they were fishermen. [17] And Jesus said to them, "Follow me and I will make you become fishers of men." [18] And immediately they left their nets and followed him. [19] And going on a little farther, he saw James the son of Zebedee and John his brother, who were in their boat mending the nets. [20] And immediately he called them; and they left their father Zebedee in the boat with the hired servants, and followed him.

In his infinite creativity, God calls each of us to know him and to serve him in a way that is unique for each individual. In the story of Jonah, God dealt with a fearful prophet who first resisted his call. When Jonah tried running from God, he found himself more in need of him than ever before (Jonah 1:1-3,11-2:1). God gave him a second chance though and, as a result of Jonah's adventures, the entire city of Nineveh was spared (3:10). When Jesus called his first disciples, they too set out on an adventure that exceeded anything they had expected (Mark 1:16-20).

In both instances, the infinite, almighty Creator reached down and called finite, created, often wounded, people to follow him—and it shook them to the core. We should not be surprised at this. In fact, we should expect this kind of activity to cause some sort of disturbance. Jonah was definitely shaken up and challenged beyond what he thought were his capabilities. The disciples also struggled for a long time to understand who Jesus was and why he had such an effect on them (Mark 6:35-37,51; 8:14-20,33; 10:25-28). In both situations, God formed those he had called into true servants—powerful witnesses to his love and mercy.

God wants each one of us to be witnesses and servants of his kingdom. No matter how well-educated or how dedicated we may be, God's call will challenge us and "shake us up." It may be as dramatic as it was for the disciples or for Jonah. It may occur over the course of many months, or even years. But God wants all of us to know the joy and the adventure of being his servants.

If we seek to be faithful to God in the little things that he calls us to each day, we will find ourselves transformed over time. He will form us into disciples who are capable of making a difference in the world, just as he formed the apostles and prophets we read about in scripture. All God is looking for are humble, open hearts.

God has surrounded each of us in his love. He has filled us with his Spirit and incorporated us into his very life. As beloved disciples, let us joyfully take up God's call to us and know that he is with us in all that we do.

Mark 1:21-28

²¹ And they went into Capernaum; and immediately on the sabbath he entered the synagogue and taught. ²² And they were astonished at his teaching, for he taught them as one who had authority, and not as the scribes. ²³ And immediately there was in their synagogue a man with an unclean spirit; ²⁴ and he cried out, "What have you to do with us, Jesus of Nazareth? Have you come to destroy us? I know who you are, the Holy One of God." ²⁵ But Jesus rebuked him, saying, "Be silent, and come out of him!" ²⁶ And the unclean spirit, convulsing him and crying with a loud voice, came out of him. ²⁷ And they were all amazed, so that they questioned among themselves, saying, "What is this? A new teaching! With authority he commands even the unclean spirits, and they obey him." ²⁸ And at once his fame spread everywhere throughout all the surrounding region of Galilee.

Mark placed this story of the cure of the man with the unclean spirit in the first chapter of his gospel to demonstrate early on the truth about who Jesus is. The people of the synagogue recognized Jesus' authority in his words; his teaching amazed them (Mark 1:22). Jesus demonstrated the authority of his words by driving out the evil spirit. As the first miracle recorded by Mark, it clearly is a sign that in Jesus' presence, the power of evil is reduced to helplessness and God's rule is supreme.

The reaction of the demon to Jesus reveals to us who Jesus is. The evil spirit recognized Jesus and twice called him by name, addressing him as "Jesus of Nazareth" and "the Holy One of God"

(Mark 1:24). To the Semitic mind, to know the name of one's enemy was to have power over him. But the demon was powerless before Jesus; in fact, the demon recognized that Jesus had "come to destroy" them (1:24). In recognizing Jesus' power, the demon, in effect, recognized Jesus as the Messiah with authority—even over evil spirits.

This should cause us to examine how we look at Jesus and his power and the extent to which we allow him to exercise it in our lives. Jesus of Nazareth is more than just an historical figure. He is the Son of God, sent into the world to restore all people to a proper relationship with God.

Do we know Jesus as the "Holy One of God" (Mark 1:24)? Can we proclaim with Peter: "We have believed, and have come to know, that you are the Holy One of God" (see John 6:69)? We can come to believe this with a rock-solid faith. Jesus has all power in heaven and on earth (see Matthew 28:18). We must ask ourselves if we acknowledge this power and authority in our lives. Do we allow him to exercise this power to heal us, to restore us to the Father, and to change our sin patterns?

We can learn from this narrative that Jesus of Nazareth is the Messiah, the one sent by God with all authority and power. We must cry out to Jesus as did the man possessed by the unclean spirit. The marvels of Jesus in the gospels witness to the reality of who he is. Let us allow scripture to teach us that Jesus is the Holy One of God and let him work in our lives.

Mark 1:29-39

²⁹ And immediately he left the synagogue, and entered the house of Simon and Andrew, with James and John. ³⁰ Now Simon's mother-in-law lay sick with a fever, and immediately they told him of her. ³¹ And he came and took her by the hand and lifted her up, and the fever left her; and she served them. ³² That evening, at sundown, they brought to him all who were sick or possessed with demons. ³³ And the whole city was gathered together about the door. ³⁴ And he healed many who were sick with various diseases, and cast out many demons; and he would not permit the demons to speak, because they knew him. ³⁵ And in the morning, a great while before day, he rose and went out to a lonely place, and there he prayed. ³⁶ And Simon and those who were with him followed him, ³⁷ and they found him and said to him, "Every one is searching for you." ³⁸ And he said to them, "Let us go on to the next towns, that I may preach there also; for that is why I came out." ³⁹ And he went throughout all Galilee, preaching in their synagogues and casting out demons.

Have you ever felt that you just couldn't get out of bed in the morning? Perhaps there was something you dreaded that was scheduled to happen that day. It may have been a job evaluation, another day of a prolonged illness, or the necessity of caring for a sick or cranky child.

Like Peter's mother-in-law who was bedridden and feverish,

we too can be weighed down by physical, emotional, or spiritual burdens. During these times of infirmity, we can become depressed, making it almost impossible for us to love and care for others. It can even become difficult to believe that God (or anyone else) cares about us.

When Jesus heard about Peter's mother-in-law, he took her by the hand and healed her. Immediately, the fever left, and she began to serve Jesus and his disciples. What power, authority, and love are manifest in Jesus' presence! There is nothing—no illness, no sin, no demon—that can stand against him.

Mark gives us this story to show us how Jesus exercised his authority through love. He loves us so much that he became a man and entered into our weak and wounded condition, triumphing over it by giving up his own life on the cross. He took on our infirmities and endured our pain. Now he invites us to receive his love and healing power. "He heals the brokenhearted, and binds up their wounds" (Psalm 147:3). Jesus wants to heal us in the deepest way possible—by increasing our capacity to accept in faith all that he did for us on the cross, by drawing us into an ever closer union with him.

Ever striving to be like his master, St. Paul sought to become all things to all people (1 Corinthians 9:22). When we believe in Jesus, partake of his mysteries at the altar, and keep his commandments, the Spirit enters into us more deeply and gives us the power to reflect Christ's love more fully. Jesus wants to rule our activities through his Spirit, moving us to love the Lord and to serve his people with humility and compassion (see Catechism of the Catholic Church, 2084).

Strengthened by the presence of the Spirit in us, let us walk in the authority and compassion of Jesus. As we do, we too will receive the ability to become all things to all people, serving them in love.

Mark 1:40-45

[40] And a leper came to him beseeching him, and kneeling said to him, "If you will, you can make me clean." [41] Moved with pity, he stretched out his hand and touched him, and said to him, "I will; be clean." [42] And immediately the leprosy left him, and he was made clean. [43] And he sternly charged him, and sent him away at once, [44] and said to him, "See that you say nothing to any one; but go, show yourself to the priest, and offer for your cleansing what Moses commanded, for a proof to the people." [45] But he went out and began to talk freely about it, and to spread the news, so that Jesus could no longer openly enter a town, but was out in the country; and people came to him from every quarter.

Mosaic law separated lepers as outcasts from the rest of the people and required them to cry out, "Unclean, unclean," when others approached (see Leviticus 13:44-46). The leper who approached Jesus directly was breaking Mosaic law. He must have deeply believed and desperately hoped that Jesus had the ability to heal him, for he said, "If you will, you can make me clean" (Mark 1:40). Not only did the leper know his need, he also had to believe that Jesus was the answer to that need. The leper would not have broken Mosaic law and approached Jesus if he had not had confidence in his compassion.

The leper represents all people before God, defiled and stained by sin. God is righteous and holy and no unclean person can dwell in his presence. All are separated from God due to sin. Even so,

God did not want his children to remain separated from him and made every provision for us to return to him through his Son, whose death and resurrection conquered sin.

We tend to think of God as far off and aloof, yet the incident of the leper testifies to God's compassion in his Son. While seeing our sin completely, he still loves us, heals us, and forgives us. His compassion comes from a oneness with humanity because his only Son became a human person and was tempted like us in every way, yet remained sinless (see Hebrews 4:15).

Jesus had no fear of the leper or of the law that required his isolation. By touching the leper, he made himself unclean in the eyes of the law. As the Son of God, however, he was free from the demands of the law. On the cross, Jesus so identified himself with sinful humanity that he touched and became our sin (2 Corinthians 5:21). When he rose from the dead, he demonstrated his power over sin.

No matter how terrible our sin or how distant we feel from God, Jesus loves us, forgives us, and wants to heal us completely. Let us seek him out with confidence as did the leper because we believe he loves us and has compassion for us. Let us approach him with true sorrow for our sins, yet without fear. If we approach him, he will stretch out his hand and touch us.

Mark 2:1-12

[1] And when he returned to Capernaum after some days, it was reported that he was at home. [2] And many were gathered together, so that there was no longer room for them, not even about the door; and he was preaching the word to them. [3] And they came, bringing to him a paralytic carried by four men. [4] And when they could not get near him because of the crowd, they removed the roof above him; and when they had made an opening, they let down the pallet on which the paralytic lay. [5] And when Jesus saw their faith, he said to the paralytic, "My son, your sins are forgiven." [6] Now some of the scribes were sitting there, questioning in their hearts, [7] "Why does this man speak thus? It is blasphemy! Who can forgive sins but God alone?" [8] And immediately Jesus, perceiving in his spirit that they thus questioned within themselves, said to them, "Why do you question thus in your hearts? [9] Which is easier, to say to the paralytic, 'Your sins are forgiven,' or to say, 'Rise, take up your pallet and walk'? [10] But that you may know that the Son of man has authority on earth to forgive sins"—he said to the paralytic— [11] "I say to you, rise, take up your pallet and go home." [12] And he rose, and immediately took up the pallet and went out before them all; so that they were all amazed and glorified God, saying, "We never saw anything like this!"

The paralytic man was so sure that Jesus would heal him that he was willing to be lifted high onto a roof by four men who were carrying his pallet, then lowered down through the roof to get close to Jesus. Jesus "saw their faith" (Mark 2:5) and worked his miracle, healing first the man's soul and then his body.

Faith, according to the book of Hebrews, "is the assurance of things hoped for, the conviction of things not seen" (Hebrews 11:1). The paralytic man and his friends did not know in advance that Jesus would heal him. But they were so convinced of his power and his love that they were willing to go to great lengths to encounter him. "Whoever would draw near to God must believe that he exists and that he rewards those who seek him" (11:6). Drawing near to God, the paralytic man received a double blessing: Absolution for his sins and strong legs.

How can we have a faith like the paralytic man? Faith is a gift—one for which we must pray. It is our first step toward God. From a position of faith, we can come to experience the joy of knowing Christ and receiving all the blessings he wants us to have. Our natural instinct is to want to know God first through our reason and intellect, and then to receive faith because we have "figured it all out." St. Anselm (c. 1033-1109) once observed: "I do not seek to understand in order to believe; but I believe in order to understand." As our faith increases, we will come to understand more about the nature of God and his work in our lives. But to develop this deeper understanding and knowledge of God, we must first believe.

Jesus performed no miracles in his hometown because of the people's lack of faith (Mark 6:5-6). Are we blocking God's power in our lives, and in the lives of our loved ones, because of our lack of faith? Let us ask the Lord to increase our faith. Jesus can banish our doubts and fears, and fill us with a faith that will open us to his mercy, his healing, and his love.

"Father, you know how weak in faith we are. Forgive us for our doubts and fears. Give us the faith that moves mountains, the faith to witness to an unbelieving world."

Mark 2:13-17

¹³ He went out again beside the sea; and all the crowd gathered about him, and he taught them. ¹⁴ And as he passed on, he saw Levi the son of Alphaeus sitting at the tax office, and he said to him, "Follow me." And he rose and followed him.
¹⁵ And as he sat at table in his house, many tax collectors and sinners were sitting with Jesus and his disciples; for there were many who followed him. ¹⁶ And the scribes of the Pharisees, when they saw that he was eating with sinners and tax collectors, said to his disciples, "Why does he eat with tax collectors and sinners?" ¹⁷ And when Jesus heard it, he said to them, "Those who are well have no need of a physician, but those who are sick; I came not to call the righteous, but sinners."

Levi was an outcast, a Jew who served the financial arm of the Roman Empire that occupied Palestine. He was probably aware that in many ways he had betrayed his people and made accommodations with the pagan culture that held them in subjection. Still, when Jesus called him, he left everything behind and followed him (Mark 2:14). This Levi is the same "Matthew" who later wrote the gospel that bears his name.

It was Levi's awareness of his position that caused him to respond so readily to the Lord. Levi knew he was sinful: He was probably reminded of it every day as he endured the scornful looks and bitter words directed at him and his form of livelihood by his own people. Perhaps he also followed the common practice among tax collectors of overcharging his clients and keeping the extra money for himself (see Luke 3:12-13). Whatever the case, Levi knew he needed a savior.

What would have been his reaction when he heard Jesus say: "Those who are well have no need of a physician, but those who are sick; I came not to call the righteous, but sinners" (Mark 2:17)? This is the wonder of our God: He calls us while we are still sinners (see Romans 5:8). Levi knew that he was spiritually sick and hard-hearted. This knowledge would have influenced him to abandon his old life and follow Jesus, the only one who could heal him.

The popular view in the world is that we are all basically good people. In the face of this philosophy, we need to remember one thing: We are all endowed with a fallen nature that has been separated from the light and life of God (see Romans 3:10-13, 23). We all seek to fulfill our own needs and desires before we even think about the desires of the Lord (see Romans 7:15, 17-20). When Levi realized this, he forsook all of his treasured things and ideas and followed Jesus. The same can also be true for us. If we ask him, the Holy Spirit will not only show us our sin, he will speak words of comfort and hope to us, calling us to Jesus, our great healer.

"Lord Jesus, you came to redeem and heal the sinful. By your Spirit, I want to experience your work in my life and learn to follow you."

Mark 2:18-22

[18] Now John's disciples and the Pharisees were fasting; and people came and said to him, "Why do John's disciples and the disciples of the Pharisees fast, but your disciples do not fast?" [19] And Jesus said to them, "Can the wedding guests fast while the bridegroom is with them? As long as they have the bridegroom with them, they cannot fast. [20] The days will come, when the bridegroom is taken away from them, and then they will fast in that day. [21] No one sews a piece of unshrunk cloth on an old garment; if he does, the patch tears away from it, the new from the old, and a worse tear is made. [22] And no one puts new wine into old wineskins; if he does, the wine will burst the skins, and the wine is lost, and so are the skins; but new wine is for fresh skins."

Something new was happening in Jesus Christ. A new order was beginning and the old was passing away. Jesus described this new relationship with God using various images. He said it was like a wedding feast where the guests rejoiced in the presence of the bridegroom (Mark 2:19). In this veiled way, Jesus was teaching the people that he was the bridegroom in their presence fulfilling the Old Testament prophecies that God would forgive his people and join himself to them as through a marriage covenant (see Hosea 2:18-20; Isaiah 62:4-5).

The parables of the wine and the cloth illustrate the newness of what was happening. Jesus creates things anew—he doesn't merely patch them up. New wine is the sign of a new era; Jesus is the one who dispenses the new wine. Christ would truly renew the whole universe. This renewal began at his birth, was fulfilled in his death and resurrection, and will be perfected in his second coming.

The church reflects the new order established by Christ and is a sign of Jesus' presence among his people. Its calling is to manifest to the world the love, harmony, peace, and unity that comes from Christ. Jesus wants his body on earth to reflect the love and unity he shares with his Father and the Holy Spirit. But this is hardly possible when his followers are divided and at odds with one another.

We should be keenly aware of our responsibility to pray that the Christian churches will be united according to the mind and heart of Christ. In our own time, disunity and division prevent the fulfillment of the new reality Christ inaugurated in his death and resurrection. We pray for unity so that the work of Christ might be fulfilled. The bridegroom cannot rejoice fully when he sees division in the people he came to gather.

"Lord Jesus, I pray that all Christians might be united according to your mind and heart. Send us your Holy Spirit to teach us to repent of our suspicions, anger, and pride. Make us one, Lord, that all the world may see the new order you came to establish."

Mark 2:23-28

23 One sabbath he was going through the grainfields; and as they made their way his disciples began to pluck ears of grain. 24 And the Pharisees said to him, "Look, why are they doing what is not lawful on the sabbath?" 25 And he said to them, "Have you never read what David did, when he was in need and was hungry, he and those who were with him: 26 how he entered the house of God, when Abiathar was high priest, and ate the bread of the Presence, which it is not lawful for any but the priests to eat, and also gave it to those who were with him?" 27 And he said to them, "The sabbath was made for man, not man for the sabbath; 28 so the Son of man is lord even of the sabbath."

The Son of man is lord even of the sabbath. (Mark 2:28)

What challenging words Jesus had for the Pharisees! They asked what seemed to be a legitimate question about the disciples' actions, which were contrary to sabbath laws. Jesus responded by confronting the smallness of their thinking about him and his ministry, and by identifying himself as lord of the sabbath.

The disciples' act of picking grain to eat was a clear violation of Jewish sabbath regulations. When the Pharisees questioned the disciples' actions, Jesus responded by revealing his authority in two ways. First, he gave the Old Testament example of David and his men eating the holy bread from the temple (1 Samuel 21:1-6), thus identifying himself with David. Just as David's men had their needs filled at the expense of strict adherence to the law, so Jesus could allow his disciples to satisfy their hunger by picking grain on the sabbath. As the Messiah prefigured by David, Jesus had the prerogative to provide for those who had left everything to accompany him in his work.

Jesus proclaimed that God created the sabbath for the benefit and welfare of human beings. Perhaps Jesus was thinking of Exodus 20:8-11 when he said, "The sabbath was made for man, not man for the sabbath" (Mark 2:27). Therefore, the law must be interpreted and observed in the light of the Lord's dual commandment of love of God and love of neighbor, which is the very spirit of the law. Jesus summed up his authority by saying that he is Lord, even of the sabbath (Mark 2:28). In doing so, he does not annul the sabbath law, but interprets it in light of his work of salvation.

This story of confrontation invites us to see the in-breaking of the kingdom of God. Just as the Pharisees' preconceptions about Jesus' ministry and the law were questioned, we too are challenged to understand that Jesus is more than just a man or a good teacher. The Son of man is Lord of all, even of the sabbath.

"Lord Jesus, help us to see your authority and lordship clearly. Break through the ways that we diminish you in our thinking. We want to live by your law of love, under your dominion."

Mark 3:1-6

¹ Again he entered the synagogue, and a man was there who had a withered hand. ² And they watched him, to see whether he would heal him on the sabbath, so that they might accuse him. ³ And he said to the man who had the withered hand, "Come here." ⁴ And he said to them, "Is it lawful on the sabbath to do good or to do harm, to save life or to kill?" But they were silent. ⁵ And he looked around at them with anger, grieved at their hardness of heart, and said to the man, "Stretch out your hand." He stretched it out, and his hand was restored. ⁶ The Pharisees went out, and immediately held counsel with the Herodians against him, how to destroy him.

This is the last in a series of five conflicts described by Mark (2:1-12; 2:13-17; 2:18-22; 2:23-28; 3:1-6) that took place between Jesus and the scribes, Pharisees, and others. This time, the final decision was made by the Pharisees to plot with the Herodians to kill Jesus (3:6). Both parties set aside their mutual hatred for one another and joined hands like brothers in order to overthrow the divine teacher, even after Jesus had shown great compassion in healing the man with the withered hand (3:5).

Most of the Pharisees were sincere people trying to live righteous lives before God. But their outward acts did not reflect transformed hearts or lead to an inner openness to God. Jesus often admonished them for this very thing, calling them "blind guides," "hypocrites," and "whitewashed tombs" (Matthew 23:24,25,27), and those who justify themselves before others (Luke 16:15). Their hearts were not transformed, and thus their acts of piety served only to glorify themselves and not God.

A disciple of Christ must go beyond the righteousness of the scribes and the Pharisees characterized by external pious acts (Matthew 5:20). He or she must be moved not with concern for external observances but with the motivations of the heart. Paul wrote of the condition of the human heart: "None is righteous, no, not one" (Romans 3:10). The only righteousness that is possible is that which is given to us by God through his grace as a free and generous gift. It is the righteousness gained through the cross of Jesus and does not come from ourselves but, rather, through faith in Jesus.

Only those who are dead to their own wills can truly follow Christ. They put aside all else to follow in the way of Jesus. It is they who can rejoice with Paul: "I have been crucified with Christ; it is no longer I who live, but Christ who lives in me; and the life I now live in the flesh I live by faith in the Son of God, who loved me and gave himself for me" (Galatians 2:20).

"Lord Jesus, by the power of your Spirit in me, help me to follow you. Help me to give you my very self."

Mark 3:7-12

[7] Jesus withdrew with his disciples to the sea, and a great multitude from Galilee followed; also from Judea [8] and Jerusalem and Idumea and from beyond the Jordan and from about Tyre and Sidon a great multitude, hearing all that he did, came to him. [9] And he told his disciples to have a boat ready for him because of the crowd, lest they should crush him; [10] for he had healed many, so that all who had diseases pressed upon him to touch him. [11] And whenever the unclean spirits beheld him, they fell down before him and cried out, "You are the Son of God." [12] And he strictly ordered them not to make him known.

A good mystery novel provides intriguing details that twist and intertwine until the reader is almost in knots. That's the point at which a good storyteller pauses; rather than adding more details, the sleuth in the story sits down to mull over the evidence. This gives the readers a chance to collect their thoughts—to assimilate what is known and to prepare for new details to come.

Mark, a master storyteller, has paused at this point to give us time for reflection. In previous chapters, we've seen Jesus healing people afflicted with one sickness after another. Jesus went out and recruited his first disciples, but soon, crowds of people were coming to him. There was that intriguing little secret that slipped out when Jesus exorcised demons: They knew who he was, but Jesus would not let them speak (Mark 1:23-26). Mark had captured the attention of his readers.

Interest was not enough in itself, however, for Mark also had a message to get across. He established a couple of general points about Jesus before proceeding with any more details or stories.

First, Jesus had overwhelming appeal for people. If you mark on a map the cities and regions from which people were coming (Mark 3:8), you would see that crowds were streaming in from all directions to listen to Jesus. He wasn't just some local teacher with a small circle of followers—he attracted great numbers of people from all places and from practically all walks of life.

Second, everyone who reads about Jesus in Mark's Gospel has to decide for himself or herself—Who is this man? What is so special about him that demons are not permitted to announce his identity? Mark would continue to give clues, but the question he wanted his audience to ponder at this point, and throughout his gospel, was: "Who is Jesus?"

Let us take time today for the reflection that Mark intended. If you're not completely convinced of the greatness and divinity of Jesus, take time today to pray about the evidence in Mark's Gospel. Those who are committed Christians—take the time today to allow the Holy Spirit to speak to you more deeply. No matter how close you've grown to Jesus, his presence always calls for change and renewal.

"Lord Jesus, I open my heart for you to speak to me. Whether you're calling for change in my personal life, or calling me to service in my family, parish, or community, I want to follow wherever you go."

Mark 3:13-19

¹³ And he went up into the hills, and called to him those whom he desired; and they came to him. ¹⁴ And he appointed twelve, to be with him, and to be sent out to preach ¹⁵ and have authority to cast out demons: ¹⁶ Simon whom he surnamed Peter; ¹⁷ James the son of Zebedee and John the brother of James, whom he surnamed Bo-anerges, that is, sons of thunder; ¹⁸ Andrew, and Philip, and Bartholomew, and Matthew, and Thomas, and James the son of Alphaeus, and Thaddaeus, and Simon the Cananaean, ¹⁹ and Judas Iscariot, who betrayed him. Then he went home.

The twelve apostles were a diverse group of people. They included uneducated fishermen; a tax collector who worked for the Roman occupying government; and Simon the Zealot, who wanted to see the Roman forces overthrown. These differences, however, took second place to the new identity these men received as disciples of Christ. No matter what their backgrounds, once they were called—and accepted their call—they became more like their Master. "And he appointed twelve, to be with him, and to be sent out to preach and have authority to cast out demons" (Mark 3:14-15).

We who call ourselves disciples of Christ are also a widely diverse collection of people. Even though we differ in many ways, what unites us is greater than what divides us. Christ living in us unifies us and strengthens us as people of God.

How do we maintain our unity as disciples in Christ? Like the first disciples, we must "be with him" (Mark 3:14). Do we set time aside out of our day to sit at the Lord's feet and listen to what he has to say? Holding on to resentments or bitterness can threaten our unity with other Christians. As God reveals them to us, we can repent of sins against unity and come to the realization that we are one in Christ. "He is before all things, and in him all things hold together" (Colossians 1:17).

Like the first disciples, we have been given the authority to proclaim the gospel from our hearts. By speaking in the name of Jesus, we can set free those bound by evil spirits. When we ardently desire to become disciples, Christ will lead us to those in need—to the poor, the sick, the lost—to all who long to hear the good news. Our specific calling may differ from the calling of other Christians, but God has a plan for each one of us. Working together with our brothers and sisters in Christ, we will be equipped to build the kingdom of God on earth.

"Lord Jesus, you called twelve apostles to yourself and now you call us. Like the apostles, we say, 'yes' to your call. Help us to build up your body."

Mark 3:20-30

20 The crowd came together again, so that they could not even eat. 21 And when his family heard it, they went out to seize him, for they said, "He is beside himself." 22 And the scribes who came down from Jerusalem said, "He is possessed by Beelzebul, and by the prince of demons he casts out the demons." 23 And he called them to him, and said to them in parables, "How can Satan cast out Satan? 24 If a kingdom is divided against itself, that kingdom cannot stand. 25 And if a house is divided against itself, that house will not be able to stand. 26 And if Satan has risen up against himself and is divided, he cannot stand, but is coming to an end. 27 But no one can enter a strong man's house and plunder his goods, unless he first binds the strong man; then indeed he may plunder his house.

28 "Truly, I say to you, all sins will be forgiven the sons of men, and whatever blasphemies they utter; 29 but whoever blasphemes against the Holy Spirit never has forgiveness, but is guilty of an eternal sin"— 30 for they had said, "He has an unclean spirit."

Each of us yearns for the healing touch of God. The long-ago moment when our first parents disobeyed God and lost his grace is somehow incorporated into the memory of each passing generation. Thus, we all cry out: "Who will save us?" The people of Jesus' time demonstrated this yearning as crowds "from Galilee . . . from Judea and Jerusalem and Idumea and from beyond the Jordan and from about Tyre and Sidon" all followed Jesus (Mark 3:7-8).

As the scribes and Pharisees watched Jesus heal and deliver the multitudes, they became angry. Perhaps they felt that their positions of respect and honor were threatened by this miracle worker. Acting out of jealousy, they tried to discredit Jesus, claiming that it was by Satan's power that he cast out demons (Mark 3:22). Jesus responded with a parable: "How can Satan cast out Satan? If a kingdom is divided against itself, that kingdom cannot stand" (3:23-24). He was not in league with Satan. Quite the contrary— Jesus was demonstrating his power over the evil one.

Genesis depicts God promising that the serpent would be defeated by the woman's offspring (Genesis 3:15). This first announcement of the gospel promised that though the struggle between good and evil would be great, Satan, the evil one, would ultimately be defeated by one like us. Jesus Christ, fully God and fully man, is the fulfillment of this promise. By his cross, he has taken away the devil's legal right to harass us and rob us of our dignity as children of God.

How can we experience the fruits of this victory? Through faith. In moments of temptation and doubt, we can pray with the psalmist, "I wait for the LORD, my soul waits, and in his word I hope" (Psalm 130:5). We can humbly confess our weakness and ask the Spirit of God to fill us with his strength. As we learn to wait for the Lord, we too will know healing and freedom.

"Lord Jesus, by your cross, you opened the way for us to know freedom. Teach us to trust in your victory over the devil. Empower us to live by faith in you, waiting for the victory you have promised."

Mark 3:31-35

[31] And his mother and his brethren came; and standing outside they sent to him and called him. [32] And a crowd was sitting about him; and they said to him, "Your mother and your brethren are outside, asking for you." [33] And he replied, "Who are my mother and my brethren?" [34] And looking around on those who sat about him, he said, "Here are my mother and my brethren! [35] Whoever does the will of God is my brother, and sister, and mother."

"Our poor beloved Don Bosco has taken leave of his senses!" So thought some of the Italian priest's colleagues as he described his ambitious plans to evangelize young people around the world. In secret, the men decided to bring him to the local asylum for treatment. A few days later, two of them came in a horse-drawn carriage to visit Bosco.

Chatting with him outside his home, they invited him on a ride through the country, hoping to lock him inside the carriage and order the driver to proceed nonstop to the asylum.

But Don Bosco, ever alert, figured out his friends' plot. As they invited him into the carriage, he graciously stepped aside, saying, "I think I still know my manners. After you." The men cautiously entered. Immediately, Don Bosco slammed the door and called to the driver: "Quick! To the asylum! You have two dangerous characters locked inside!" It took the two priests the rest of the day to convince the doctors that they were not the intended patients.

In a similar way, members of Jesus' family wanted to spare him (and perhaps themselves) from any further embarrassment as his ministry grew and his words took on deeper and darker meanings. They sought him out to try to restrain him. But with one statement, Jesus disarmed their arguments (Mark 3:33-35)—God's will was to be obeyed, whatever the cost, however radical or difficult it might seem.

Do we try to control God? Do we fear that he might call us to go farther than we want to go? Perhaps he wants us to reconcile a broken relationship, or perhaps he wants us to be more generous with our resources or our lives. Or, are we trying to control others who are giving up more of their lives to serve Christ? Are we fearful that they are becoming too radical, embarrassing themselves . . . and us? How often do we stifle the Spirit in these ways? How often do we want to protect ourselves from the very God whose love drove him to the cross?

Of course, we must be discerning. Sometimes wisdom may call for caution or patience. Yet, we must ask whether we are motivated by something other than love and reverence for Christ. Let us seek to follow and obey him completely, echoing his prayer, "Your will be done, On earth as it is in heaven" (Matthew 6:10).

Parables and Miracles

MARK
4–5

Mark 4:1-20

[1] Again he began to teach beside the sea. And a very large crowd gathered about him, so that he got into a boat and sat in it on the sea; and the whole crowd was beside the sea on the land. [2] And he taught them many things in parables, and in his teaching he said to them: [3] "Listen! A sower went out to sow. [4] And as he sowed, some seed fell along the path, and the birds came and devoured it. [5] Other seed fell on rocky ground, where it had not much soil, and immediately it sprang up, since it had no depth of soil; [6] and when the sun rose it was scorched, and since it had no root it withered away. [7] Other seed fell among thorns and the thorns grew up and choked it, and it yielded no grain. [8] And other seeds fell into good soil and brought forth grain, growing up and increasing and yielding thirtyfold and sixtyfold and a hundredfold." [9] And he said, "He who has ears to hear, let him hear."

[10] And when he was alone, those who were about him with the twelve asked him concerning the parables. [11] And he said to them, "To you has been given the secret of the kingdom of God, but for those outside everything is in parables; [12] so that they may indeed see but not perceive, and may indeed hear but not understand; lest they should turn again, and be forgiven." [13] And he said to them, "Do you not understand this parable? How then will you understand all the parables? [14] The sower sows the word. [15] And these are the ones along the path, where the word is sown; when they hear, Satan immediately comes and takes away the word which is sown in them. [16] And these in like manner are the ones sown upon rocky ground, who, when they hear the word, immediately receive it with joy; [17] and they have no root in themselves, but endure for a while; then, when tribulation or persecution arises on account of the word, immediately they fall

away. [18] And others are the ones sown among thorns; they are those who hear the word, [19] but the cares of the world, and the delight in riches, and the desire for other things, enter in and choke the word, and it proves unfruitful. [20] But those that were sown upon the good soil are the ones who hear the word and accept it and bear fruit, thirtyfold and sixtyfold and a hundred-fold."

In first-century Palestine, it was common for farmers to sow their seed first, and then go back and plow the soil. In this way, the seed could be mixed in with different types of soil, and some hard or rocky patches of soil could be broken up and soft-ened, helping the seed to bear greater fruit. While some of the soil may not be the most fertile at the beginning of the process, by the end, it has a far greater chance of supporting the life and fruitful-ness of the seed it has received.

In a similar way, none of us should think that because we see hardness or difficulties in our lives now, that we are beyond hope of change, or that it's too late for us. God can "plow" us up at any time, making us more receptive to the work he has sown in us and more able to bear the abundant fruit that his seed is capable of producing. We should always keep our eyes and ears open, looking for ways that God may be trying to work a greater soften-ing in our hearts, a greater receptivity to his word.

Jesus told his disciples that the seed is God's word, a living word that finds its expression not only in scripture, but also in the church's sacred tradition and in the witness of men and women throughout history whose lives speak profoundly of the power of

Christ's resurrection. When this seed is sown and the soil is prepared to receive it, great things happen.

Lives are restored to their original innocence and openness to God. Relationships are healed. Long-standing resentments and crippling fears are rooted out. Entire families are transformed, and even whole villages and towns are deeply affected. The weak become strong, the timid become courageous, the arrogant become humble, and the oppressive become servants. There is no limit to what can happen, because Christ, "the first fruits of those who have fallen asleep" (1 Corinthians 15:20), has been raised from the dead and has poured out a grace that truly renews the whole world.

"Heavenly Father, thank you for lavishing the seed of your word in our lives. By your Spirit, fill us with a sense of gratitude and expectation for everything you want to accomplish in us, both individually and as your church. Lord, may our lives bear the abundant fruit of righteousness and peace."

Mark 4:21-25

[21] And he said to them, "Is a lamp brought in to be put under a bushel, or under a bed, and not on a stand? [22] For there is nothing hid, except to be made manifest; nor is anything secret, except to come to light. [23] If any man has ears to hear, let him hear." [24] And he said to them, "Take heed what you hear; the measure you give will be the measure you get, and still more will be given you. [25] For to him who has will more be given; and from him who has not, even what he has will be taken away."

Scripture is the inspired word of God. Through it, God reveals truths about his kingdom and the intentions of his heart. It contains the knowledge we need to live lives that are worthy of the calling we have received. God intends that the meaning of his word be understood, not concealed: "There is nothing hid, except to be made manifest; nor is anything secret, except to come to light" (Mark 4:22).

God wants his truth to be known—he does not want to conceal it from us. The more we are open to the truth, the more we will understand it. Jesus said, "To him who has will more be given; and from him who has not, even what he has will be taken away" (Mark 4:25). It is not that Christ is taking away from us the understanding of his kingdom; it is that the more we are attached to our human ideas and ways of thinking, the less we will understand his ways. In effect, we can close ourselves off from understanding.

God can change our hearts and minds as we seek him daily and open ourselves to him. "The measure you give will be the measure you get, and still more will be given you" (Mark 4:24). As we give our minds to the Lord, we will receive ever greater understanding back from him. The most effective way to open our minds to God is through prayer and scripture reading. As we do these things with open hearts, we allow the Holy Spirit to teach us the truth. He enlightens our minds so that the fullness of the truth becomes clear.

Through prayer and scripture reading, we meet God face to face. At work, pause from time to time and ask God to direct you in your business dealings. At home, seek God as you relate to your spouse and raise your children. Students need to seek God's face in relating to friends and dealing with peer pressure. The more we seek God in all situations, the more we will understand the truth.

"Father in heaven, I seek your face today. Through the power of the Holy Spirit, open my eyes to the deeper meaning of the scriptures. Conceal nothing from me. I seek your face in all I do today, at home and at work. Change my heart, dear Lord, that I may know your truth."

Mark 4:26-34

26 And he said, "The kingdom of God is as if a man should scatter seed upon the ground, 27 and should sleep and rise night and day, and the seed should sprout and grow, he knows not how. 28 The earth produces of itself, first the blade, then the ear, then the full grain in the ear. 29 But when the grain is ripe, at once he puts in the sickle, because the harvest has come."
30 And he said, "With what can we compare the kingdom of God, or what parable shall we use for it? 31 It is like a grain of mustard seed, which, when sown upon the ground, is the smallest of all the seeds on earth; 32 yet when it is sown it grows up and becomes the greatest of all shrubs, and puts forth large branches, so that the birds of the air can make nests in its shade."
33 With many such parables he spoke the word to them, as they were able to hear it; 34 he did not speak to them without a parable, but privately to his own disciples he explained everything.

It is possible to understand a bit more about faith in God by considering how farmers live. To ensure a good harvest, they need to plant good seed at the right time, keep their fields free of competing weeds and harmful insects, and gather their crops properly when they ripen. As much as they try to control these factors, farmers are ultimately dependent upon God for more fundamental things—the land, good soil, rain, sufficient light, and warmth.

Farmers know they must work hard, but they also know that growth is something that takes place almost independently of their efforts. Until the advent of powerful chemical fertilizers and irrigation to enhance growth, all farmers could basically do was cooperate with life and growth. The fact that it happened was a mystery in which they trusted, but which they could barely speed up or force.

The farm-oriented parables in Mark teach us to recognize these things as we consider growth in our spiritual lives. Growth depends on God; it is usually gradual and is sometimes imperceptible to us. Because God himself is concerned about us, however, we should expect that he will lead us in paths that promote genuine and abundant fruit. Our expectancy should be based on our knowledge that growth is something God himself desires and attends to.

Once the seed is sown, God cares for the growth. Through the work of the Spirit, growth comes from within us. Like the farmer, we can nurture this growth by removing the thorns and thistles in our lives. We can make the decisions to avoid the things that hamper God's work in us—certain books and television programs, angers and festering resentments, concern only for ourselves and our interests, indifference to the poor and suffering. We can nourish the seed of our faith through reading God's word, prayer, and the Eucharist. Gradually, with sufficient time, we will see this seed spring to life—perhaps without really knowing when it happened.

If we allow God to work in us, we will grow—even though we may not be aware of it at the time. The seeds in these parables are meant to show that great things come from small beginnings. This is God's promise from all time:

> On the mountain height of Israel will I plant it, that it may bring forth boughs and bear fruit, and become a noble cedar; and under it will dwell all kinds of beasts; in the shade of its branches birds of every sort will nest. (Ezekiel 17:23)

Mark 4:35-41

[35] On that day, when evening had come, he said to them, "Let us go across to the other side." [36] And leaving the crowd, they took him with them in the boat, just as he was. And other boats were with him. [37] And a great storm of wind arose, and the waves beat into the boat, so that the boat was already filling. [38] But he was in the stern, asleep on the cushion; and they woke him and said to him, "Teacher, do you not care if we perish?" [39] And he awoke and rebuked the wind, and said to the sea, "Peace! Be still!" And the wind ceased, and there was a great calm. [40] He said to them, "Why are you afraid? Have you no faith?" [41] And they were filled with awe, and said to one another, "Who then is this, that even wind and sea obey him?"

W e can imagine the disciples' panic as the water began to rise in the boat. Besides being vast and powerful, the sea is also unpredictable. When a storm rises, even a short distance from shore can seem like miles. Throughout scripture, the surging power of the sea has been used to represent the forces of chaos and darkness in the world—images we read of in the telling of the great flood (Genesis 7:17-24) and the mythic sea creature, Leviathan (Psalm 74:13-14; Isaiah 27:1).

Despite the turbulent seas, Jesus was not only calm, but fast asleep. When the disciples woke him and asked: "Teacher, do you not care if we perish?" it appears that they knew he could do something but were concerned about his seeming indifference. As we read of the many times that the disciples had to learn to place their trust in Jesus, we can be greatly encouraged. They had already seen Jesus deliver a demon-possessed man (Mark 1:21-27), heal a paralytic (2:1-12), and restore a man's withered hand (3:1-5), yet they still feared that he would not save them. Here we begin to appreciate Jesus' words: "Why are you afraid? Have you no faith?" (Mark 4:40).

This miracle was yet another sign to the disciples (and to us) that Jesus is always aware and concerned—no matter how bleak the circumstances may look. The fact that the forces of nature responded so quickly to his rebuke showed his complete sovereignty—even over something as powerful as a raging sea. The storm didn't just become manageable, "a great calm" resulted immediately (Mark 4:39).

Jesus is always with us, especially during the storms of life. On the cross and in his resurrection, he not only triumphed over the powers of darkness, he defeated death itself, our ultimate enemy. Now risen in glory, he offers us countless opportunities to cast our cares on him and let him deliver us. Through challenge after challenge, he seeks to deepen our trust in his love and provision. In hope, let us surrender our lives to him.

"Lord Jesus, we believe that you care for us, even in the midst of chaos and confusion. Help us to abandon our lives to you and trust that you will bring us safely into your kingdom."

Mark 5:1-20

[1] They came to the other side of the sea, to the country of the Gerasenes. [2] And when he had come out of the boat, there met him out of the tombs a man with an unclean spirit, [3] who lived among the tombs; and no one could bind him any more, even with a chain; [4] for he had often been bound with fetters and chains, but the chains he wrenched apart, and the fetters he broke in pieces; and no one had the strength to subdue him. [5] Night and day among the tombs and on the mountains he was always crying out, and bruising himself with stones. [6] And when he saw Jesus from afar, he ran and worshiped him; [7] and crying out with a loud voice, he said, "What have you to do with me, Jesus, Son of the Most High God? I adjure you by God, do not torment me." [8] For he had said to him, "Come out of the man, you unclean spirit!" [9] And Jesus asked him, "What is your name?" He replied, "My name is Legion; for we are many." [10] And he begged him eagerly not to send them out of the country. [11] Now a great herd of swine was feeding there on the hillside; [12] and they begged him, "Send us to the swine, let us enter them." [13] So he gave them leave. And the unclean spirits came out, and entered the swine; and the herd, numbering about two thousand, rushed down the steep bank into the sea, and were drowned in the sea. [14] The herdsmen fled, and told it in the city and in the country.

And people came to see what it was that had happened.
[15] And they came to Jesus, and saw the demoniac sitting there,
clothed and in his right mind, the man who had had the legion;
and they were afraid. [16] And those who had seen it told what had
happened to the demoniac and to the swine. [17] And they began
to beg Jesus to depart from their neighborhood. [18] And as he was
getting into the boat, the man who had been possessed with
demons begged him that he might be with him. [19] But he refused,
and said to him, "Go home to your friends, and tell them how
much the Lord has done for you, and how he has had mercy on
you." [20] And he went away and began to proclaim in the
Decapolis how much Jesus had done for him; and all men
marveled.

His exile was terrible: No one but the dead to talk to—no
voices except those of the inner temptations, accusations,
and rages that taunted him day and night. His torment
was so bad that his only relief—and it was temporary at that—
came from hurting himself physically to take his mind off his inte-
rior anguish. His neighbors sometimes tried to intervene, but their
methods—chains and isolation—only increased his misery. Worse
yet, he found that in his times of deepest darkness he possessed an
unnatural strength and was capable of even greater violence.

Then, on one stormy night, while his shrieking matched the
howling of the winds, he sensed a different presence. Without any
warning, the storm suddenly stopped (Mark 4:37,39). It didn't
taper off gradually—it ceased. A boat pulled up and some men

stepped ashore. One man in particular caught his attention, and he wondered, "How could anyone have survived such a storm?" There wasn't time to ponder this. He knew somehow within himself that he had to meet this man. He sensed that this stranger offered him a hope that he didn't even dare dream about—release.

Even as he was bounding toward the man, the all too familiar voices started up again with an intensity he'd never before experienced. He felt as if the inner cacophony would undo him. Desperately wanting to know this man's peace, yet utterly terrified of what might happen to him as a result, he threw himself at the man's feet and babbled out a confused mixture of threats and supplication.

After a few moments charged with tension and power, something broke within him—he was free! The entire weight of his torment was lifted, and the disturbing voices were silenced— drowned in the sea; the man in front of him was looking down at him with a gentle smile. Later, clothed with dignity and restored to rationality, he was sent to tell others about his deliverance and the one who had done this for him. He would tell them that restoration was available to everyone. They didn't have to be as desperate and as violent as he had been. They only had to reach out to this man, and they too would be filled and comforted.

"Jesus, we want to know your peace. Fill us with your life and deliver us from any darkness that keeps us from receiving your love. Set us free, Lord."

Mark 5:21-43

²¹ And when Jesus had crossed again in the boat to the other side, a great crowd gathered about him; and he was beside the sea. ²² Then came one of the rulers of the synagogue, Jairus by name; and seeing him, he fell at his feet, ²³ and besought him, saying, "My little daughter is at the point of death. Come and lay your hands on her, so that she may be made well, and live." ²⁴ And he went with him.

And a great crowd followed him and thronged about him. ²⁵ And there was a woman who had had a flow of blood for twelve years, ²⁶ and who had suffered much under many physicians, and had spent all that she had, and was no better but rather grew worse. ²⁷ She had heard the reports about Jesus, and came up behind him in the crowd and touched his garment. ²⁸ For she said, "If I touch even his garments, I shall be made well." ²⁹ And immediately the hemorrhage ceased; and she felt in her body that she was healed of her disease. ³⁰ And Jesus, perceiving in himself that power had gone forth from him, immediately turned about in the crowd, and said, "Who touched my garments?" ³¹ And his disciples said to him, "You see the crowd pressing around you, and yet you say, 'Who touched me?' " ³² And he looked around to see who had done it. ³³ But the woman, knowing what had been done to her, came in fear and trembling and fell down before him, and told him the whole truth. ³⁴ And he said to her, "Daughter, your faith has made you well; go in peace, and be healed of your disease."

³⁵ While he was still speaking, there came from the ruler's house some who said, "Your daughter is dead. Why trouble the Teacher any further?" ³⁶ But ignoring what they said, Jesus said to the ruler of the synagogue, "Do not fear, only believe." ³⁷ And he allowed no one to follow him except Peter and James and John

the brother of James. [38] When they came to the house of the ruler of the synagogue, he saw a tumult, and people weeping and wailing loudly. [39] And when he had entered, he said to them, "Why do you make a tumult and weep? The child is not dead but sleeping." [40] And they laughed at him. But he put them all outside, and took the child's father and mother and those who were with him, and went in where the child was. [41] Taking her by the hand he said to her, "Talitha cumi"; which means, "Little girl, I say to you, arise." [42] And immediately the girl got up and walked; for she was twelve years old. And immediately they were overcome with amazement. [43] And he strictly charged them that no one should know this, and told them to give her something to eat.

J airus, a man of considerable eminence in his own town, came and fell at Jesus' feet, asking in faith for him to heal his daughter (Mark 5:22-24). In the incident that followed, when Jesus asked who had touched him, the hemorrhaging woman also came and fell at his feet, describing what had happened to her as the result of her faith (5:26-28). The people dispatched by Jairus from his household, on the other hand, showed little faith, doubting that Jesus had power over death (5:35).

Where do we stand? How do we look at Jesus? Is he some wonder-worker of the past? Was he perhaps a very holy man, an outstanding combination of generosity and humility? How deeply do we believe that Jesus Christ is the eternal Son of God, our perfect and complete salvation? Many of our attitudes about faith and the Christian life are formed by the world, and if we were to look around, it would become clear to us that this world functions with little recourse to faith. Yet, it is this environment that often forms our thoughts about God.

When we act in envy or bitterness, does this not signify a lack of faith? Are we not, in effect, saying: "I have a right to be angry because nobody (not even God) is looking after my interests"? When we repent of a specific sin, but resign ourselves to the fact that we will probably go ahead and commit it again, is this not a sign that we do not believe that Jesus' blood has cleansed us and won us freedom from sin? When we find ourselves restless in scripture or prayer, is it not oftentimes because we don't expect that Jesus will speak to us and give us peace and joy in his presence?

These are but a few of the many ways in which our unbelief can manifest itself. Jesus wants us to put aside thoughts like these so that our faith can become more like that of Jairus and the hemorrhaging woman. He wants to tell us, "Do not fear, only believe" (Mark 5:36). He can say this only if we have begun to put off our old attitudes and mind sets and take on a new mind that is formed in his image. We need to come before God in humility today and ask him to increase our faith. Let us renounce the attitudes of the world and beg the Holy Spirit to fill us with his truth instead.

Jesus Misunderstood and Rejected

MARK
6:1–7:23

Mark 6:1-6

¹ He went away from there and came to his own country; and his disciples followed him. ² And on the sabbath he began to teach in the synagogue; and many who heard him were astonished, saying, "Where did this man get all this? What is the wisdom given to him? What mighty works are wrought by his hands! ³ Is not this the carpenter, the son of Mary and brother of James and Joses and Judas and Simon, and are not his sisters here with us?" And they took offense at him. ⁴ And Jesus said to them, "A prophet is not without honor, except in his own country, and among his own kin, and in his own house." ⁵ And he could do no mighty work there, except that he laid his hands upon a few sick people and healed them. ⁶ And he marveled because of their unbelief.

And he went about among the villages teaching.

The people of Nazareth were amazed at Jesus and his teaching. Yet despite his wisdom and the miraculous deeds he worked, they did not believe and "took offense at him" (Mark 6:3). Jesus "could do no mighty work there . . . . And he marveled because of their unbelief" (Mark 6:5-6). The Greek word used in this passage for unbelief is *apistian*. It is the opposite of *pistis*, which means faith. By examining the biblical meaning of *pistis*, we can better understand the unbelief of the Nazareans.

Faith involves our relationship with God, the way we speak to him and listen to him. When he heard the promises of God,

Abraham "believed the LORD; and he [God] reckoned it to him as righteousness" (Genesis 15:6). Because Abraham put his faith in the word of God, he experienced God's work. In the same way, when Jesus speaks to us in scripture or in our prayer and we believe him, we too will know his presence and work in our lives.

Faith calls for obedience to God. As we obey him out of love, God can work in our lives. Jesus told his disciples, "If you love me, you will keep my commandments" (John 14:15). When we believe or have faith, we put ourselves under God and submit to him.

To be obedient to God's word, we have to trust and hope in him. In Hebrews 11, for example, the writer gave example after example of the holy men and women in the Old Testament who, because of their faith, persevered in following the Lord, trusting that his word was reliable. They could place their hope in God, knowing that he would be true to all his promises.

Obedience, trust, and hope are essential parts of faith. When confronted by Jesus' words and deeds, the people of Nazareth did not believe. Because the people there would not submit to Christ and obey him, and because they had no trust and hope in him, Jesus could not work among them. Let us pray that we will believe in Jesus and will experience his presence and work among us.

"Holy Spirit, increase in me my faith in Jesus. Enable me to place my trust and hope in the Father and to obey his Son's words. Spirit, I want to know the power of God in my life. I believe—help my unbelief."

Mark 6:7-13

[7] And he called to him the twelve, and began to send them out two by two, and gave them authority over the unclean spirits. [8] He charged them to take nothing for their journey except a staff; no bread, no bag, no money in their belts; [9] but to wear sandals and not put on two tunics. [10] And he said to them, "Where you enter a house, stay there until you leave the place. [11] And if any place will not receive you and they refuse to hear you, when you leave, shake off the dust that is on your feet for a testimony against them." [12] So they went out and preached that men should repent. [13] And they cast out many demons, and anointed with oil many that were sick and healed them.

What an exciting moment for the apostles! Jesus called them and sent them out to begin the mission for which he had chosen them. The twelve apostles were those who were to carry on the mission of Jesus, performing works similar to those in Jesus' own ministry: Preaching, teaching repentance, expelling demons, and anointing and healing the sick (Mark 6:12-13).

The apostles had been very close to Jesus throughout his early ministry, observing his miracles, hearing his teaching, and even benefiting from his personal explanation of the parables he told. This intimate time of preparation was meant to equip the Twelve to be sent out as Jesus' authorized representatives, bringing his life to the world. In fact, the Greek word *apostolos*, translated "apostle," means an ambassador or one who is sent out.

The closeness of fellowship that the Twelve enjoyed with Jesus, and the responsibility he conferred on them makes, even more puzzling the fact that they still often failed to understand who he was. The seeds of this misunderstanding could be seen earlier when the apostles failed to understand Jesus' parables and were dumbfounded at his calming of the storm (Mark 4:35-41). This juxtaposition of the apostles' favored position and their lack of understanding is clear throughout the Gospel of Mark. It finally becomes evident that true understanding of Jesus comes only through the effects of his death and resurrection and the sending of the Spirit.

In recognition of their human weakness, Jesus gave specific instruction to the Twelve regarding their mission. He admonished them not to make provisions for themselves, but to rely on God and the hospitality of those who would hear and accept their words. He stressed dependence on God and the urgency of the apostles' missionary work (Mark 6:8-10). This stands in contrast to our normal tendency to provide for ourselves and to rely on our own resources, even when attempting to serve God and do his work. Our human condition is such that we try to control God and have him fit into our lives and plans.

"Come, Holy Spirit. Open our minds and hearts and give us a deeper understanding of who Jesus is and a desire to take up the work he has given us. Help us to release control of our lives that we might more fully trust in the Father and his care for us."

Mark 6:14-29

[14] King Herod heard of it; for Jesus' name had become known. Some said, "John the baptizer has been raised from the dead; that is why these powers are at work in him." [15] But others said, "It is Elijah." And others said, "It is a prophet, like one of the prophets of old." [16] But when Herod heard of it he said, "John, whom I beheaded, has been raised." [17] For Herod had sent and seized John, and bound him in prison for the sake of Herodias, his brother Philip's wife; because he had married her. [18] For John said to Herod, "It is not lawful for you to have your brother's wife." [19] And Herodias had a grudge against him, and wanted to kill him. But she could not, [20] for Herod feared John, knowing that he was a righteous and holy man, and kept him safe. When he heard him, he was much perplexed; and yet he heard him gladly. [21] But an opportunity came when Herod on his birthday gave a banquet for his courtiers and officers and the leading men of Galilee. [22] For when Herodias' daughter came in and danced, she pleased Herod and his guests; and the king said to the girl, "Ask me for whatever you wish, and I will grant it." [23] And he vowed to her, "Whatever you ask me, I will give you, even half of my kingdom." [24] And she went out, and said to her mother, "What shall I ask?" And she said, "The head of John the baptizer." [25] And she came in immediately with haste to the king, and asked, saying, "I want you to give me at once the head of John the Baptist on a platter." [26] And the king was exceedingly sorry; but because of his oaths and his guests he did not want to break his word to her. [27] And immediately the king sent a soldier of the guard and gave orders to bring his head. He went and beheaded him in the prison, [28] and brought his head on a platter, and gave it to the girl; and the girl gave it to her mother. [29] When his disciples heard of it, they came and took his body, and laid it in a tomb.

The embodiment of radicalism, John the Baptist dressed in camel's hair, "ate locusts and wild honey" (Mark 1:6), and prepared the way for Jesus by boldly exhorting people to repent and be baptized for the forgiveness of sins (Mark 1:4). All during his life, John stood as a prefigurement of Jesus, the one he heralded. An angel foretold both of their births and named both of them (Luke 1:13,31; Isaiah 49:1). They were both conceived as a result of God's miraculous intervention (Luke 1:24-25,35). Even in infancy, people recognized God's hand upon them (Luke 1:66; 2:18-19).

Both John and Jesus "grew and became strong in spirit," and each spent time alone before beginning his public ministry (Luke 1:80; 2:40; Mark 1:12-13). The Lord made both their mouths like sharp swords (Isaiah 49:2) able to cut through the deceptions of human reasoning with the truths of repentance, forgiveness, and God's loving call to bear "fruits that befit repentance" (Luke 3:8; Matthew 7:21). John willingly suffered and died for Christ—"the way, and the truth, and the life" (John 14:6)—just as Christ died so that all people could become children of God (John 1:12; Romans 8:14).

Of John the Baptist, St. Bede the Venerable said, "Such was the quality and strength of the man who accepted the end of this present life by shedding his blood." Though he was "locked away in the darkness of prison . . . [he] deserved to be called a bright and shining lamp" by Christ, "the Light of life" (*Homilies*, 23).

As the Holy Spirit's temples, we too are called to be bright lights, glorifying Christ in a world darkened by sin (Matthew 5:16). Although we probably will not experience martyrdom, we can daily imitate Christ by following the Spirit's guidance instead of the inclinations of the flesh. Our radicalness may result in suffering, but our hearts will overflow with joy as the Spirit enables us (like Jesus) to triumph over death. Despite difficulties, we will rejoice as we see Jesus reborn into the world through our witness.

"God our Father, you called John the Baptist to be the herald of your Son's birth and death. As he gave his life in witness to truth and justice, so may we strive to profess our faith in your gospel" (Opening Prayer commemorating the Beheading of John the Baptist).

Mark 6:30-34

30 The apostles returned to Jesus, and told him all that they
had done and taught. 31 And he said to them, "Come away by
yourselves to a lonely place, and rest a while." For many were
coming and going, and they had no leisure even to eat. 32 And
they went away in the boat to a lonely place by themselves.
33 Now many saw them going, and knew them, and they ran
there on foot from all the towns, and got there ahead of them.
34 As he landed he saw a great throng, and he had compassion on
them, because they were like sheep without a shepherd; and he
began to teach them many things.

J esus was more than just a teacher; he cared for his disciples. He did not burden them with more duties and responsibilities than they could bear. He was aware of their condition and knew how to provide them with rest and relaxation as well as instruction and correction. Jesus' loving and tender care extended beyond his disciples, however, to embrace all people. We see this heart of love in his response to the crowds. Even though he had intended to rest, Jesus decided to teach them instead because he saw that "they were like sheep without a shepherd" (Mark 6:34).

Jesus is the Shepherd sent by the Father to care for us. In him, we are not "scattered" and "driven away" (Jeremiah 23:1-6), but gathered and tended to. This is why the crowds came to him in the first place. Hearing about how Jesus expressed his love in powerful yet tender ways attracted them. The wonderment of seeing miracles, hearing him teach, and experiencing his care was far better than seeing any great performer.

The good news is that Jesus Christ is the same today. He still delights in teaching and caring for his people, especially those who have no one to care for them. He may not be physically present, but he has put his Holy Spirit in us to teach us all things (John 14:26). It is through the Spirit that God reconciles our ways to his ways and forms a deep friendship with each of us.

Through daily prayer and scripture reading, we too will be attracted to Jesus. We will want his guidance, and we will confide in him our joys and sorrows. Jesus, the Good Shepherd, will do for us today what he did for the crowds so long ago. Let us never tire of turning to him. There is no barrier too large for him to overcome (Ephesians 2:14). He is always ready to bless, to heal, and to forgive.

"Jesus, we gather before you as sheep who need your protection and tender care. Guide us this day as tirelessly as you guided the disciples. We trust that you will provide for all of our needs."

Mark 6:35-44

[35] And when it grew late, his disciples came to him and said, "This is a lonely place, and the hour is now late; [36] send them away, to go into the country and villages round about and buy themselves something to eat." [37] But he answered them, "You give them something to eat." And they said to him, "Shall we go and buy two hundred denarii worth of bread, and give it to them to eat?" [38] And he said to them, "How many loaves have you? Go and see." And when they had found out, they said, "Five, and two fish." [39] Then he commanded them all to sit down by companies upon the green grass. [40] So they sat down in groups, by hundreds and by fifties. [41] And taking the five loaves and the two fish he looked up to heaven, and blessed, and broke the loaves, and gave them to the disciples to set before the people; and he divided the two fish among them all. [42] And they all ate and were satisfied. [43] And they took up twelve baskets full of broken pieces and of the fish. [44] And those who ate the loaves were five thousand men.

Who was this Jesus, who could draw vast crowds into a remote part of the country just to be with him? What were they seeking from him that they would travel so far from their homes with nothing to eat? Mark explains that Jesus "had compassion on them . . . and he began to teach them many things" (Mark 6:34). It was Jesus' teaching that attracted them—his descriptions of the kingdom of God that filled their hearts with hope and expectation.

As evening came, the disciples asked Jesus to send the people away for food. It's interesting that the people themselves did not make this request; they seemed content just to listen to Jesus. Wanting to continue to care for the people, Jesus fed them miraculously—all 5,000 of them. First he gave them teaching and then gave them bread—food for the soul and food for the body; food for the spiritual life and food for the earthly life.

Scripture, God's word to us, is the "bread" that we need (Matthew 4:3-4)—the "food" that satisfies us beyond our imagination (Wisdom 16:26). Everyday we make sure we eat to satisfy our physical hunger. Likewise, each of us possesses spiritual hunger, a hunger that can only be satisfied by God's word.

St. John Chrysostom (c. 347-407) encouraged his people to come to Jesus in this way:

> Let us therefore learn ourselves to wait upon Jesus . . . to cling continually to the things of the Spirit. Let us seek the heavenly bread, and having received it let us cast away all worldly cares. For if those people left their homes and towns and families following Jesus into the wilderness, and didn't leave when they became hungry, how much more ought we, when approaching such a table, to show more self-control and set our love on the things of the Spirit. (*On the Gospel of Matthew*, Homily 49)

When we read scripture, we can be refreshed as if by a cold drink on a hot day. We can be sustained like a tired laborer by a hearty meal. We can be nourished like a growing child by milk. Imagine the joy Jesus must have felt feeding all of those people with the miraculous bread. Surely he rejoices in the same way today when one of us picks up his word and is nourished by it.

Mark 6:45-52

⁴⁵ Immediately he made his disciples get into the boat and go before him to the other side, to Bethsaida, while he dismissed the crowd. ⁴⁶ And after he had taken leave of them, he went into the hills to pray. ⁴⁷ And when evening came, the boat was out on the sea, and he was alone on the land. ⁴⁸ And he saw that they were distressed in rowing, for the wind was against them. And about the fourth watch of the night he came to them, walking on the sea. He meant to pass by them, ⁴⁹ but when they saw him walking on the sea they thought it was a ghost, and cried out; ⁵⁰ for they all saw him, and were terrified. But immediately he spoke to them and said, "Take heart, it is I; have no fear."
⁵¹ And he got into the boat with them and the wind ceased. And they were utterly astounded, ⁵² for they did not understand about the loaves, but their hearts were hardened.

Mark's Gospel continues to present to us evidence that shows who the Christ really is. We saw Jesus' power in multiplying the loaves and fishes. Even so, his disciples "did not understand about the loaves, but their hearts were hardened" (Mark 6:52). Now we witness Jesus' command over the powers of nature as he walks on water and stills the raging wind.

There is more at stake here than just a show of power. The Old Testament refers to walking on water as a divine function. In the Book of Job, for example, Job declared, "[God] alone stretched out the heavens, and trampled the waves of the sea" (Job 9:8). By walking on water, Jesus revealed his divinity. This manifestation of God is enhanced by Mark's mysterious statement: "He meant to pass by them" (Mark 6:48). This is reminiscent of the Lord passing by Moses in Exodus 33:19-22. Explicit or implied, the account of Jesus walking on water is a testimony that he is God.

It is not surprising, therefore, to read that the disciples were utterly astounded, even terrified, at what they saw. How reassuring were Jesus' calm words: "It is I; have no fear" (Mark 6:50). Jesus brings that same reassurance to all who are fearful. Have you ever turned yourself over to Jesus and let him comfort you? In his presence, we learn there is nothing to fear. We begin to see the truth of this as we submit our lives to him and trust in him. As we allow him to be the Lord of our lives, he reveals greater things to us. In the same way, the revelation of the Christ child in Bethlehem did not end there but led to even greater revelation throughout Jesus' life and in his death and resurrection.

Does the violence in the world frighten us? Are we apprehensive about financial matters? Do health problems weigh heavily on us? Let us recall Jesus' words: "It is I; have no fear." Commenting on Jesus' walking on water, St. Augustine wrote: "He came treading the waves; and so he puts all the swelling tumults of life under his feet. Christians—why be afraid?"

Mark 6:53-56

[53] And when they had crossed over, they came to land at Gennesaret, and moored to the shore. [54] And when they got out of the boat, immediately the people recognized him, [55] and ran about the whole neighborhood and began to bring sick people on their pallets to any place where they heard he was. [56] And wherever he came, in villages, cities, or country, they laid the sick in the market places, and besought him that they might touch even the fringe of his garment; and as many as touched it were made well. ▩▩▩

Have you noticed how in Mark's Gospel, when people heard that Jesus had arrived in a certain place, they *ran* to him. They did not walk to see Jesus, they *ran* to see him. They *ran* to the other side of the lake to listen to him (Mark 6:33), and when he returned, they *ran* to bring the sick to him (6:55). When he returned from the mountain where he was transfigured, the people *ran* to him again (9:15), and later, the rich young man *ran* up to him (10:17).

The people ran because they were powerfully drawn to Jesus. They saw that he was able to heal and to teach them, and it attracted them. They earnestly longed for what he offered: Words of hope and comfort, revelation about the love of the Father, and the power of a humble, surrendered life. They ran just to *see* him heal the sick. There was an urgency: We must go to Jesus now!

Jesus never turned anyone away. He was always open to the people's needs. It was so simple! Jesus loved and cared for those he met. People simply ran to Christ to get their needs met!

When Mark wrote that those who even touched the hem of Jesus' garment were healed, he used the Greek word *sozo*, which also means to be delivered or saved. The physically sick who Jesus touched (like the paralytic in Mark 2:1-12) knew that their healing was not just physical but spiritual as well—their sins were forgiven and their hearts were touched and transformed by the love of the Father (2:5). Similarly, those who ran to Jesus were drawn not only by the reports of physical healings, but also by the stories of inner healings—people being "saved" from their sin and from spiritual sickness. Everyone, including the physically healthy, had cause to run after this spiritual healing! Let us also run to Jesus and seek his healing power.

"Lord Jesus, you are the mighty healer, filled with compassion for your people. You call us to come to you in faith so that we can be healed and saved. Jesus, we come to you eagerly. Lord, save us!"

Mark 7:1-13

[1] Now when the Pharisees gathered together to him, with some of the scribes, who had come from Jerusalem, [2] they saw that some of his disciples ate with hands defiled, that is, unwashed. [3] (For the Pharisees, and all the Jews, do not eat unless they wash their hands, observing the tradition of the elders; [4] and when they come from the market place, they do not eat unless they purify themselves; and there are many other traditions which they observe, the washing of cups and pots and vessels of bronze.) [5] And the Pharisees and the scribes asked him, "Why do your disciples not live according to the tradition of the elders, but eat with hands defiled?" [6] And he said to them, "Well did Isaiah prophesy of you hypocrites, as it is written, 'This people honors me with their lips, but their heart is far from me; [7] in vain do they worship me, teaching as doctrines the precepts of men.' [8] You leave the commandment of God, and hold fast the tradition of men."

[9] And he said to them, "You have a fine way of rejecting the commandment of God, in order to keep your tradition! [10] For Moses said, 'Honor your father and your mother'; and, 'He who speaks evil of father or mother, let him surely die'; [11] but you say, 'If a man tells his father or his mother, What you would have gained from me is Corban' (that is, given to God)— [12] then you no longer permit him to do anything for his father or mother, [13] thus making void the word of God through your tradition which you hand on. And many such things you do."

The Pharisees who confronted Jesus about his disciples' ritual purity were so concerned with strict observance of the law— some of which didn't even come from God—that they lost sight of God's desire for mercy, justice, and love. More than anything else, such inverted priorities caused Jesus to respond abruptly and forcefully as he directed his disciples to look at the state of their hearts before they considered their actions.

When we look at Jesus' description of the human heart and the sins that rise from it (see Mark 7:20-21), we might feel a sense of self-condemnation and despair. After all, who could look at such a list without seeing something of a reflection of their own inner state?

God calls us to examine our hearts not so that we would feel condemned, but so that we would know freedom and peace. Many saints have commented that the more deeply they saw their sin, the more fully they recognized God's mercy and love. The humility they demonstrated was no cowardice, but a recognition of their need for God, coupled with confidence in his power at work in them. In fact, they considered it a privilege to come to such self-knowledge, for it always led them to the Lord. It was this privilege that these Pharisees denied themselves and prevented their followers from experiencing.

Through his cross, Jesus has forgiven our sins. He shed his blood to cleanse our hearts. We don't have to be perfect to be accepted by God. We simply have to respond to him by repenting of our sins, loving him in return, and choosing with a willing heart to obey him. Jesus will take care of the rest. Looking into our hearts is not such a painful experience when we realize that in the midst of the sin and darkness, Jesus is still there, wanting to shine his light more brightly.

"Lord, by your cross you conquered sin. In your resurrection you removed condemnation. May these truths give us the freedom to examine our hearts and know the power of your Spirit as we seek to please you and obey your commands."

Mark 7:14-23

¹⁴ And he called the people to him again, and said to them, "Hear me, all of you, and understand: ¹⁵ there is nothing outside a man which by going into him can defile him; but the things which come out of a man are what defile him." ¹⁷ And when he had entered the house, and left the people, his disciples asked him about the parable. ¹⁸ And he said to them, "Then are you also without understanding? Do you not see that whatever goes into a man from outside cannot defile him, ¹⁹ since it enters, not his heart but his stomach, and so passes on?" (Thus he declared all foods clean.) ²⁰ And he said, "What comes out of a man is what defiles a man. ²¹ For from within, out of the heart of man, come evil thoughts, fornication, theft, murder, adultery, ²² coveting, wickedness, deceit, licentiousness, envy, slander, pride, foolishness. ²³ All these evil things come from within, and they defile a man."

Have you ever noticed how radiant people look when they're in love? You can often read what's going on in their hearts just by looking at their faces. In a similar way, our actions often reveal our attitudes. It's not hard to view a person's everyday life and begin to understand how he or she feels about certain political or social issues, or even about God. Some people may be very quiet about their inner lives, but the love and peace of Christ still shine through, whether they're changing a flat tire, buying food at the market, or running a business meeting. Conversely, others may "do" all the right things but somehow lack the liveliness of a relationship with Christ.

The Pharisees were expert at instituting and adhering to regulations based on ancient traditions. Yet, for some of them, their hearts were far from the God of their ancestors. In a similar way, we may confuse ritual piety with true godliness, or observance of traditions with inner purity. When observance is looked upon as an end in itself, and not as a reflection of a love and reverence for God, we have missed out on the life of joy and peace promised by Christ.

It's easy to believe that a wall of separation exists between our hearts and our bodies, between our inner selves and our actions. But God made us as unified persons, with bodies designed to express what is in our hearts, and hearts intimately tied up with our relationships in the world. God is concerned with our hearts; he takes a deep interest in the way we relate to one another. If we detect in our relationships any of the vices Jesus mentioned—covetousness, lust, envy, slander, or pride (Mark 7:21-22)—we need to understand that they are reflections of a heart that needs purification by the Lord. If we allow these vices into our relationships with others, we continue to bring impurity to our hearts.

Jesus said that the greatest commandment is to love God wholeheartedly and to love our neighbor as ourselves (Mark 12:28-31). When such love is our primary concern, we are on the road to purity of heart—we derive life and nourishment from our observances and relate to others in sincerity and love. Let us ask the Spirit to search us today and help us to see how we can respond to God more deeply and love one another more genuinely.

The Messiah Among the Gentiles

Mark 7:24-30

[24] And from there he arose and went away to the region of Tyre and Sidon. And he entered a house, and would not have any one know it; yet he could not be hid. [25] But immediately a woman, whose little daughter was possessed by an unclean spirit, heard of him, and came and fell down at his feet. [26] Now the woman was a Greek, a Syrophoenician by birth. And she begged him to cast the demon out of her daughter. [27] And he said to her, "Let the children first be fed, for it is not right to take the children's bread and throw it to the dogs." [28] But she answered him, "Yes, Lord; yet even the dogs under the table eat the children's crumbs." [29] And he said to her, "For this saying you may go your way; the demon has left your daughter." [30] And she went home, and found the child lying in bed, and the demon gone.

J esus went off to the territory of Tyre and Sidon. This was gentile territory, about forty miles northwest of Nazareth on the coast of the Mediterranean Sea in the province of Phoenicia. The woman who approached him was identified as a Gentile by religion and birth. ("Greek" signifies Gentile by religion; "Syrophoenician," one by birth.)

Jesus' venture into this territory was a testimony that he had come for all people, Jew and Gentile alike. It might seem to us from his exchange of words with the woman that he was discriminating against her by referring to Gentiles as "dogs." In Jewish usage at the time, "dogs" was a common term for Gentiles. Jesus was testing the woman's desire and determination.

The woman approached Jesus with both great need and deep belief. She fell at his feet and begged him to heal her daughter. Her response to Jesus' words (Mark 7:28) gave evidence that she was hungering for what Jesus could do. The Lord honored her faith and healed her daughter.

Everyone needs Jesus. It makes no difference what one's race, nationality, creed, or background may be. He accepts everyone who comes to him; he rejects no one. The gospel is not exclusive. All who seek Jesus sincerely will find him and be filled by him. Do we have a faith like this woman's that would enable us to approach Jesus and ask to be fed?

This passage challenges our work of evangelization. Do we see all as equal in their need for Christ? Are we too selective in deciding with whom we will share the gospel? It does not matter whether a person is unappealing to us, or doesn't seem open to Jesus because of his or her lifestyle. Jesus wants every person for his own. We must keep this in mind as we proclaim the gospel message of salvation in Jesus.

"Come, Holy Spirit. Help us to know our need for Jesus—the only one who can heal and free us. Lead us as we share the truth of the gospel of Jesus Christ with others. Give us the confidence and the words to proclaim the truth of Jesus and the glory of the Father's kingdom."

Mark 7:31-37

[31] Then he returned from the region of Tyre, and went through Sidon to the Sea of Galilee, through the region of the Decapolis. [32] And they brought to him a man who was deaf and had an impediment in his speech; and they besought him to lay his hand upon him. [33] And taking him aside from the multitude privately, he put his fingers into his ears, and he spat and touched his tongue; [34] and looking up to heaven, he sighed, and said to him, "Ephphatha," that is, "Be opened." [35] And his ears were opened, his tongue was released, and he spoke plainly. [36] And he charged them to tell no one; but the more he charged them, the more zealously they proclaimed it. [37] And they were astonished beyond measure, saying, "He has done all things well; he even makes the deaf hear and the dumb speak."

First century Jews did not have a single, agreed-upon expectation of what the Messiah would be like. Many did feel that his influence would be over the whole world, not just over Israel. And many commonly felt that the Messiah would bring an end to history and the world as they knew it, ushering in a wonderful age in which God would reign.

When the crowd saw Jesus healing the deaf and mute man, they took this as a sign that the Messiah had come, and they saw a glimmer of the glorious future that awaited Israel. He fulfilled the words of the prophet: "Then the eyes of the blind shall be opened, and the ears of the deaf unstopped; then shall the lame man leap like a hart, and the tongue of the dumb sing for joy" (Isaiah 35:5-6).

Jesus was careful to clarify what his coming meant. He was not a king who would take dominion over the earth. He had not come to bring an end to history. However, his coming *did* bring the kingdom of God to fruition. In all his miracles, Jesus always did everything well (see Mark 7:37), exhibiting his authority over all creation and all evil. By healing the deaf and mute man, Jesus showed that the kingdom of God was upon us. Most of all, by dying and rising to new life, Jesus showed us heaven—that God *did* have a plan for us that extended beyond the grave and the way there was now open.

Let us spend some time today rejoicing at what Jesus' coming has meant for us. If we neglect his presence, we can get bogged down in the problems or details of the day. Before long we can begin to think that God doesn't do great things for us today, or that he really doesn't make that big a difference in our lives. Let us repent of our unbelief and open our hearts to God with expectations of great and divine things.

"Lord Jesus, help me to recall and recount the wonders you have accomplished in my life and throughout the history of your people. Unstop my ears so that your words will resound in my memory. Your kingdom is truly at hand, and I long for the day when your work in me is complete."

Mark 8:1-10

¹ In those days, when again a great crowd had gathered, and they had nothing to eat, he called his disciples to him, and said to them, ² "I have compassion on the crowd, because they have been with me now three days, and have nothing to eat; ³ and if I send them away hungry to their homes, they will faint on the way; and some of them have come a long way." ⁴ And his disciples answered him, "How can one feed these men with bread here in the desert?" ⁵ And he asked them, "How many loaves have you?" They said, "Seven." ⁶ And he commanded the crowd to sit down on the ground; and he took the seven loaves, and having given thanks he broke them and gave them to his disciples to set before the people; and they set them before the crowd. ⁷ And they had a few small fish; and having blessed them, he commanded that these also should be set before them. ⁸ And they ate, and were satisfied; and they took up the broken pieces left over, seven baskets full. ⁹ And there were about four thousand people. ¹⁰ And he sent them away; and immediately he got into the boat with his disciples, and went to the district of Dalmanutha.

Mark's account of the feeding of the 4,000 is basically the same as the earlier story of the feeding of the 5,000 (see Mark 6:35-44). It is different, however, in some very important ways. The first account among the 5,000 took place in Jewish territory. This one took place among the Gentiles. Some biblical scholars believe that Mark retold the same story in a different way to teach his readers about the mission of Jesus to the Gentiles as well as to the Jews.

In this story, the disciples had less to do with the miracle than in the earlier version where Jesus challenged them to perform the miraculous (Mark 6:37). In the second feeding narrative, Jesus took it upon himself to provide his people with the bread they needed to emphasize more clearly how people are totally dependent upon him. The disciples had witnessed the earlier miracle, yet they asked, "How can one feed these men with bread here in the desert?" (8:4). This seeming contradiction (the disciples would have known the answer having been present at the first feeding) occurs because Mark wanted, once again, to point his readers to Jesus as the one who provides for all their needs. He is the bread of life (John 6:35).

Mark also made it clear that this miracle took place "in the desert" (Mark 8:4), far away from any town or civilization. This was to illustrate that the Gentiles were a people who had "come a long way" (Mark 8:3, see also Joshua 9:6,9 and 2 Chronicles 6:32), and who occupied a barren land. The Gentiles, who did not live under the covenant that God had made with the Israelites, were also invited to partake of the grace that Jesus came to bring. They were not to be excluded from the fellowship with God that had been promised to the Israelites. Jesus came to save all, not just a select few.

The miracle Jesus worked feeding the 4,000 was intended to bring Gentiles to him. It contains a message to us as well: Jesus wants a people. He will gather them from east to west, from Jew and Gentile. Will we respond to his call and come to him to be fed?

Jesus and the Twelve: Discipleship

MARK
8:11–10:52

Mark 8:11-13

[11] The Pharisees came and began to argue with him, seeking from him a sign from heaven, to test him. [12] And he sighed deeply in his spirit, and said, "Why does this generation seek a sign? Truly, I say to you, no sign shall be given to this generation." [13] And he left them, and getting into the boat again he departed to the other side.

Because we know Jesus is God, we may tend to overlook the fact that, as a man, he experienced all the human reactions and emotions that we do. We may be surprised at the frustration expressed in the phrase, "He sighed deeply in his spirit" (Mark 8:12). But Jesus could read hearts (Luke 9:47). He knew that the Pharisees' demand for a sign was born not from a search for truth, but "to test him" (Mark 8:11). Here, Jesus is revealed as one who is like us in all things, even in frustrating conflicts with the unbelieving religious leaders of his day.

In the Old Testament, God strengthened the faith of his people with the memory of past signs (such as the Exodus), by providing them with signs in the present, and by encouraging them with prophecy of future signs. Many of the people and their leaders expected the messianic days to provide signs and wonders at least equal to those in the Exodus. Such expectations were generally connected with dreams of victory over the pagans.

Jesus may have disappointed such expectations from the human point of view, but he fulfilled them perfectly from the spiritual point of view. He inaugurated true salvation in the signs of his miracles and the great sign of his being lifted up in glory on the cross. Unlike the Israelites in the desert, Jesus refused to tempt God by asking for signs on his own account, or to satisfy those who asked for signs in order to test him.

Can we see anything of ourselves in the attitude of those who asked Jesus for a sign? What are our expectations from Jesus' salvific mission? Do we acknowledge his saving death and resurrection as the supreme sign in our lives? Or do we seek to put him to the test by demanding signs that suit us, rather than trusting him and acknowledging our total dependence on him? Do we truly believe his words that the "Father knows what you need before you ask him" (Matthew 6:8)? Do our lives show that kind of trust?

Let us renew our commitment to trust totally in the Father's love, the Son's redeeming sacrifice, and the Spirit's sanctifying work. We need no other sign.

Mark 8:14-21

[14] Now they had forgotten to bring bread; and they had only one loaf with them in the boat. [15] And he cautioned them, saying, "Take heed, beware of the leaven of the Pharisees and the leaven of Herod." [16] And they discussed it with one another, saying, "We have no bread." [17] And being aware of it, Jesus said to them, "Why do you discuss the fact that you have no bread? Do you not yet perceive or understand? Are your hearts hardened? [18] Having eyes do you not see, and having ears do you not hear? And do you not remember? [19] When I broke the five loaves for the five thousand, how many baskets full of broken pieces did you take up?" They said to him, "Twelve." [20] "And the seven for the four thousand, how many baskets full of broken pieces did you take up?" And they said to him, "Seven." [21] And he said to them, "Do you not yet understand?"

The disciples continued in their inability to understand what Jesus had been trying to teach them as he preached and worked miracles in Galilee and the Decapolis (Mark 6:6–8:21). Jesus had multiplied the bread and fishes, walked on water, healed the sick in Gennesaret and the child of the Syrophoenician woman, and cured a deaf man. Despite all these wonderful signs of God's power, the disciples—like the Pharisees who asked for a sign (Mark 8:11)—still did not understand.

Jesus, deeply troubled by the disbelief he had been encountering, left with his disciples to go to the other side of the lake. As they were enroute, Jesus cautioned them not to be like the

Pharisees who demanded signs despite the evidence of God in their midst. He warned them "of the leaven of the Pharisees and the leaven of Herod" (Mark 8:15). As used here, this leaven symbolized something with a strong inner corrupting power. It was an evil influence that could spread like an infection and destroy the whole body. Jesus was cautioning the disciples against allowing their lack of understanding to harden into cynicism and disbelief as it had in some of the religious leaders.

Jesus questioned the disciples at length (Mark 8:17-21). Despite having been with him and having witnessed his miraculous power, their understanding was still flawed. They failed to grasp the significance of who Jesus was and what he was doing. Jesus chided them for this: "Having eyes do you not see, and having ears do you not hear?" (Mark 8:18). In doing this, he echoed the words of the prophet Isaiah, whom God had sent to speak a message of repentance to Israel (Isaiah 6:9-10). Jesus' final question was: "Do you not yet understand?" (Mark 8:21).

This account of Jesus' relationship with his disciples challenges us to evaluate our own understanding of God's work in our lives and in the world. Too often we can be like the Pharisees and disciples and miss out on the fullness of God's life among us. We can allow lack of understanding to let us become cynical and unbelieving. Let us ask the Holy Spirit to make the life of Jesus a living reality in us.

"Come, Holy Spirit. Give us the gift of understanding. Open our eyes that we might see; open our ears that we might hear; open our hearts that we might believe."

Mark 8:22-26

²² And they came to Bethsaida. And some people brought to him a blind man, and begged him to touch him. ²³ And he took the blind man by the hand, and led him out of the village; and when he had spit on his eyes and laid his hands upon him, he asked him, "Do you see anything?" ²⁴And he looked up and said, "I see men; but they look like trees, walking." ²⁵ Then again he laid his hands upon his eyes; and he looked intently and was restored, and saw everything clearly. ²⁶ And he sent him away to his home, saying, "Do not even enter the village."

W hy was the blind man of Bethsaida healed in stages, rather than all at once? Jesus laid his hands on the man's eyes, and he saw, but his vision was blurred. Again Jesus laid hands on the man's eyes, and this time his sight was restored completely.

The man's more gradual return to sight reflects the gradual journey of Jesus' disciples from spiritual blindness to spiritual insight. Surely they had seen Jesus perform many signs and wonders. Peter later confessed that Jesus was the Christ (Mark 8:29). Yet, as Jesus began to reveal to them what was going to happen—that he would suffer and die—the disciples struggled to comprehend God's plan for redemption. "And Peter took him, and began to rebuke him" (8:32). They still lacked the spiritual acuity to grasp God's plan for the salvation of the world through Jesus.

Many of us have come to the Lord gradually, through repeated encounters with him in prayer, in the liturgy, in the sacraments, and in others who reflect Christ. With each successive encounter, our spiritual blindness is reduced and we begin to see God for who he really is. With each encounter, we come to accept God's plan for our lives, and to comprehend that this plan is more wonderful than anything mankind could have designed. Once the blind man's eyes were healed, he "saw everything clearly" (Mark 8:25). Christ wants us to see clearly as well, and we can do so through his gentle healing touch.

Like the blind man, we can beg Jesus to touch us (Mark 8:22). The Lord did not reject the blind man, nor will he reject us. As we emerge from our spiritual blindness and are freed from the sin that clouds our vision, we can light the path to Christ for others as well. We can have "the mind of Christ" (1 Corinthians 2:16). We can become better able to discern God's will for our lives and more sensitive to the voice of the Lord as he prompts us to follow him.

"Lord Jesus, touch us and transform our spiritual blindness into a clear vision of you and your call for us. Heal our woundedness and brokenness. Forgive us for our sinful ways. 'For with you is the fountain of life; in your light do we see light' (Psalm 36:9)."

Mark 8:27-33

27 And Jesus went on with his disciples, to the villages of Caesarea Philippi; and on the way he asked his disciples, "Who do men say that I am?" 28 And they told him, "John the Baptist; and others say, Elijah; and others one of the prophets." 29 And he asked them, "But who do you say that I am?" Peter answered him, "You are the Christ." 30 And he charged them to tell no one about him.

31 And he began to teach them that the Son of man must suffer many things, and be rejected by the elders and the chief priests and the scribes, and be killed, and after three days rise again. 32 And he said this plainly. And Peter took him, and began to rebuke him. 33 But turning and seeing his disciples, he rebuked Peter, and said, "Get behind me, Satan! For you are not on the side of God, but of men."

The disciples journeying with Jesus into the villages around Caesarea Philippi must have been excited and expectant as a result of witnessing so many physical healings and miracles. They recognized that Jesus possessed unusual powers, and Peter could rightly claim, "You are the Christ" (Mark 8:29). Yet Jesus knew they had little understanding of his ministry, of who he was, and of why he had come among them.

By questioning his apostles about what people thought about him, Jesus opened up a way to teach them the true nature of his mission: "The Son of man must suffer many things, and be rejected by the elders and the chief priests and the scribes, and be killed, and after three days rise again" (Mark 8:31).

Jesus truly was the Messiah, not an earthly king as some of his followers envisioned, but the suffering servant (Isaiah 53:12). Christ's way is the way of the cross. His sacrifice is the sacrifice of his own life to free us from sin. He invites us to follow him by denying ourselves, taking up our crosses, and surrendering our lives for his sake and the sake of the gospel (Mark 8:34-35).

The apostles and disciples—hearing these words of Jesus— must have been somewhat uneasy at the challenge they faced. We too, though believing them to be true, may prefer not to hear them or hope they don't touch us in a very personal way. But if we wish to follow Christ, we too will suffer. We must die to sin and that requires suffering because sin is so deeply rooted in us.

The patterns of sin that so often dominate our lives—anger, jealousies, resentments, untruths, and deceitful practices—have all been put to death by the cross of Christ: "And you, who were dead in trespasses . . . God made alive together with him" (Colossians 2:13). The victory has already been won. When tempted to sin, we must acknowledge our need to die to self, deny ourselves the satisfaction of holding on to our sin, and claim Christ's victory on the cross over every sinful tendency.

If we accept the challenge to die and rise with Christ, we will become his faithful followers. In this, he will be our help: "The Lord GOD helps me; therefore I have not been confounded . . . he who vindicates me is near . . . . Behold, the Lord GOD helps me" (Isaiah 50:7-9).

Mark 8:34–9:1

[34] And he called to him the multitude with his disciples, and said to them, "If any man would come after me, let him deny himself and take up his cross and follow me. [35] For whoever would save his life will lose it; and whoever loses his life for my sake and the gospel's will save it. [36] For what does it profit a man, to gain the whole world and forfeit his life? [37] For what can a man give in return for his life? [38] For whoever is ashamed of me and of my words in this adulterous and sinful generation, of him will the Son of man also be ashamed, when he comes in the glory of his Father with the holy angels."

[1] And he said to them, "Truly, I say to you, there are some standing here who will not taste death before they see the kingdom of God come with power."

Jesus' exhortation to anyone who would be his follower to "deny himself and take up his cross and follow me" (Mark 8:34) was as difficult for the people of his day to accept as it is for us today. No one likes to be confronted with stark choices between eternal life and eternal condemnation, yet this is what Christ said we must face. Our tendency is to seek out some intermediate path between the holy and the worldly that allows us to enjoy maximum benefits while paying the minimum price. We do not want to renounce our ways, take up our cross, and follow Jesus.

We can see this attitude reflected in various aspects of our lives. Some seek out riches and power, regardless of the cost to others, and refuse to accept any social, moral, or spiritual accountability for their actions. Even in our churches, many people seek a Christianity that offers comfort, consolation, and peace of mind, yet feel no call to love others in any meaningful way. We like to hear that we are forgiven, but hate to hear that we must change our ways, forgive others, and "sin no more" (John 5:14).

In our daily choices, we either seek the path of least resistance or become so obsessed with one particular facet of life that we can see nothing else. In all of these examples, we cut ourselves off from following Christ in the way that leads to eternal life. Jesus wants us to seek to conquer this attitude, for it will condemn us to spiritual emptiness and eternal separation from God.

Christ has not promised us an easy life. We all must face difficult choices about what we will do with the life that has been given to us. Christ calls us to embrace the life that *he* chose, one in which he sought only to do the Father's will, to love others, and to give himself for the kingdom of God. It was the way of the cross. In the world's eyes, Jesus' life and death may have seemed a useless waste.

Jesus calls us to share his life, to renounce our own ways, to embrace the cross, and to follow him. He calls us to an active, practical, and dedicated life in which God's will is prayerfully sought out and implemented, regardless of cost. We are given the opportunity, as individuals and as the body of Christ on earth, to walk as Christ did along the path to eternal life.

Mark 9:2-13

[2] And after six days Jesus took with him Peter and James and John, and led them up a high mountain apart by themselves; and he was transfigured before them, [3] and his garments became glistening, intensely white, as no fuller on earth could bleach them. [4] And there appeared to them Elijah with Moses; and they were talking to Jesus. [5] And Peter said to Jesus, "Master, it is well that we are here; let us make three booths, one for you and one for Moses and one for Elijah." [6] For he did not know what to say, for they were exceedingly afraid. [7] And a cloud overshadowed them, and a voice came out of the cloud, "This is my beloved Son; listen to him." [8] And suddenly looking around they no longer saw any one with them but Jesus only.

[9] And as they were coming down the mountain, he charged them to tell no one what they had seen, until the Son of man should have risen from the dead. [10] So they kept the matter to themselves, questioning what the rising from the dead meant. [11] And they asked him, "Why do the scribes say that first Elijah must come?" [12] And he said to them, "Elijah does come first to restore all things; and how is it written of the Son of man, that he should suffer many things and be treated with contempt? [13] But I tell you that Elijah has come, and they did to him whatever they pleased, as it is written of him."

Jesus had begun to teach his disciples who he was and what it meant to be called disciples. Having forewarned them of his impending death and resurrection (Mark 8:31), he called

Peter, James, and John aside to offer them a glimpse of the glory that was to come. The announcement of his suffering and resurrection perplexed the disciples and raised troubling questions in their minds. Through the transfiguration, Jesus reassured them, strengthening their belief by a divine revelation that gave a glimpse of the future heavenly kingdom.

This revelation was important. Jesus had told his followers that they were to walk in the way he walked; to take up their cross just as he would; to become like their master (Mark 8:34-39). Lest they focus morbidly on suffering and death, he showed them a little of the glorious life that awaits those who follow him faithfully. Such a preview was meant to refresh the disciples and encourage them to continue on with Jesus.

St. Anastasius of Sinai urged all Christians: "Become like Peter, caught up in the vision, drawn away from this world and from earthly attractions. Leave the flesh behind and turn to the Creator, to who Peter said in ecstasy: 'Lord, it is good for us to be here' " (*Sermon on the Transfiguration of the Lord*). It is good for *us* to be there too, caught up with the Lord, drawn away from the attractions and cares of the world. We are disciples of Jesus, learning continually what it means to follow him. We need to be taught by Jesus daily. We must "listen to God's voice summoning us from the mountaintop. . . . We must hasten [there] as Jesus did" (Anastasius, *Sermon*). We must be instructed, comforted, and refreshed and, thus, experience even now a share of the fullness we will know when Jesus comes again in glory.

Every day God calls us to be renewed by his Son—in the Eucharist, in our times of prayer, through reading scripture, and as we sit quietly in his presence. "Indeed, it is good to be with Jesus and to remain [there] forever" (Anastasius, *Sermon*). Amid the many occupations, toil, confusion, and struggles of our days, it is indeed good to be with Jesus. The world offers comforts and consolations, but none that imparts peace and joy as richly and enduringly as does intimacy with God. "What greater happiness than to be with God, to be like him, to live in the light?" (Anastasius, *Sermon*).

Mark 9:14-29

[14] And when they came to the disciples, they saw a great crowd about them, and scribes arguing with them. [15] And immediately all the crowd, when they saw him, were greatly amazed, and ran up to him and greeted him. [16] And he asked them, "What are you discussing with them?" [17] And one of the crowd answered him, "Teacher, I brought my son to you, for he has a dumb spirit; [18] and wherever it seizes him, it dashes him down; and he foams and grinds his teeth and becomes rigid; and I asked your disciples to cast it out, and they were not able." [19] And he answered them, "O faithless generation, how long am I to be with you? How long am I to bear with you? Bring him to me." [20] And they brought the boy to him; and when the spirit saw him, immediately it convulsed the boy, and he fell on the ground and rolled about, foaming at the mouth. [21] And Jesus asked his father, "How long has he had this?" And he said, "From childhood. [22] And it has often cast him into the fire and into the water, to destroy him; but if you can do anything, have pity on us and help us." [23] And Jesus said to him, "If you can! All things are possible to him who believes." [24] Immediately the father of the child cried out and said, "I believe; help my unbelief!" [25] And when Jesus saw that a crowd came running together, he rebuked the unclean spirit, saying to it, "You dumb and deaf spirit, I command you, come out

of him, and never enter him again." [26] And after crying out and convulsing him terribly, it came out, and the boy was like a corpse; so that most of them said, "He is dead." [27] But Jesus took him by the hand and lifted him up, and he arose. [28] And when he had entered the house, his disciples asked him privately, "Why could we not cast it out?" [29] And he said to them, "This kind cannot be driven out by anything but prayer and fasting."

J esus lived every moment with radical, childlike trust in the Father. His total dependence gave him the power to do God's will always.

Mark placed the miracle of the possessed boy within the broader context of the final journey to Jerusalem. It not only illustrated the authority of Jesus, but also revealed another dimension of discipleship. When the father of the possessed boy approached Jesus, he revealed a shaky, half-hearted hope: "*If* you can do anything, have pity on us and help us" (Mark 9:22). Jesus challenged his attitude with a promise: "All things are possible to him who believes" (Mark 9:23). It was an invitation to share in Jesus' own abiding trust in God. The man's response set an example for all Christians who struggle with their faith: "I believe; help my unbelief!" (Mark 9:24). Because the man responded with honesty, Jesus proceeded to heal his son.

In addition to its lesson about faith, the story reverberates with an eschatological tone as well, displaying Mark's sense of the tension between the "now present" and the "not yet" aspect of the kingdom of God. The Twelve had previously been commissioned by Jesus and had successfully exorcised demons (Mark 6:13). However, they failed in their effort to cast this spirit out of the boy (Mark 9:18). Jesus explained: "This kind cannot be driven out by anything but prayer and fasting" (Mark 9:29). He thus indicated that the disciples needed to grow in belief, even though they had experienced a portion of God's reign. Mark wanted his readers to realize that they, like the Twelve, were called to develop a mature faith as they waited for the kingdom of God to come in its fullness.

Mark's account also included an echo of the resurrection. The boy, after Jesus delivered him, appeared "like a corpse" (Mark 9:26). Jesus "took him by the hand and lifted him up" (Mark 9:27). In the original Greek language, Mark's terminology fore-shadowed Jesus' resurrection and hinted at another aspect of dis-cipleship: Christians may sometimes feel powerless and lifeless, but beginning even now, Jesus delivers us and raises us to new life, a work that will be completed on the last day.

"Lord Jesus, we long to taste the fullness of your kingdom. Help us to believe more deeply in you, so that we may be grounded in a mature trust and be able to witness to the reality of your presence among us."

Mark 9:30-37

[30] They went on from there and passed through Galilee. And he would not have any one know it; [31] for he was teaching his disciples, saying to them, "The Son of man will be delivered into the hands of men, and they will kill him; and when he is killed, after three days he will rise."

[32] But they did not understand the saying, and they were afraid to ask him. [33] And they came to Capernaum; and when he was in the house he asked them, "What were you discussing on the way?" [34] But they were silent; for on the way they had discussed with one another who was the greatest. [35] And he sat down and called the twelve; and he said to them, "If any one would be first, he must be last of all and servant of all." [36] And he took a child, and put him in the midst of them; and taking him in his arms, he said to them, [37] "Whoever receives one such child in my name receives me; and whoever receives me, receives not me but him who sent me."

The Son of man will be delivered into the hands of men, and they will kill him; and when he is killed, after three days he will rise.
(Mark 9:31)

The cross of Jesus will always confront us with the question: "Why did Jesus have to die and rise from the dead?" In order to understand the cross, we need teachable minds that are open to the work of the Holy Spirit. "For the word of the cross is folly to those who are perishing, but to us who are being saved it is the power of God" (1 Corinthians 1:18). Only the Spirit of God can teach us about the cross and its power for our lives. Our human minds, unaided by spiritual enlightenment, will reject the truth of the cross as folly.

The cross of Jesus was central to his mission. We can see by the nature of the disciples' concerns (Mark 9:33-35), however, that they were oblivious to the centrality of the cross in Jesus' mission.

Instead, they remained intent on their own pursuits in this life as they discussed who was the greatest among them (Mark 9:34).

How are we to understand the meaning of the cross and embrace it in our own lives? Jesus' words about humility give us a clue: "If any one would be first, he must be last of all and servant of all" (Mark 9:35). We must become like Christ if we are to understand the cross: "Though he was in the form of God, [he] did not count equality with God a thing to be grasped, but emptied himself, taking the form of a servant, being born in the likeness of men" (Philippians 2:6-7).

To come to Jesus like children does not mean to return to the ignorance and naiveté of childhood. Rather, it means to embrace Christ and his cross as "the power of God and the wisdom of God" (1 Corinthians 1:24) for it is the means to our salvation. Paul was faithful in preaching "Christ crucified" (1:23) for he knew that "the foolishness of God is wiser than men, and the weakness of God is stronger than men" (1:25). As we are humble—even as little children (Mark 9:36-37)—and dependent on God, we will turn from our human reasoning and be open to the wisdom of God concerning the cross of Christ.

Mark 9:38-48

[38] John said to him, "Teacher, we saw a man casting out demons in your name, and we forbade him, because he was not following us." [39] But Jesus said, "Do not forbid him; for no one who does a mighty work in my name will be able soon after to speak evil of me. [40] For he that is not against us is for us. [41] For

truly, I say to you, whoever gives you a cup of water to drink because you bear the name of Christ, will by no means lose his reward. [42] "Whoever causes one of these little ones who believe in me to sin, it would be better for him if a great mill-stone were hung round his neck and he were thrown into the sea. [43] And if your hand causes you to sin, cut it off; it is better for you to enter life maimed than with two hands to go to hell, to the unquenchable fire. [45] And if your foot causes you to sin, cut it off; it is better for you to enter life lame than with two feet to be thrown into hell. [47] And if your eye causes you to sin, pluck it out; it is better for you to enter the kingdom of God with one eye than with two eyes to be thrown into hell, [48] where their worm does not die, and the fire is not quenched.

How difficult Jesus' teaching can be for our modern minds to grasp! Imagine cutting off your hand or plucking out your eye to prevent yourself from sinning. Yet, the more subtle point behind his words is humility. It is easy for us to become complacent or to think of ourselves as better than others. But Jesus taught that his disciples are not to look down on others who may not seem as "Christian" as they do, yet who still love God. We are not to become so proud of our identity as Christians that we lose vigilance against our fallen nature or the lies of the Devil.

How do we maintain a disposition of humility? By continually asking the Spirit to show us how deeply we need Jesus. We often try to stop sinning by our own efforts rather than drawing close to

Jesus, the source of all power. At the root of all pride is a self-sufficiency that is foreign to the gospel. It is the very thing that moved Adam and Eve to break God's command: They tried to become like God, but without God.

Our redemption should astound us. How comforting to realize that it is *Jesus* who saves us, not our attempts to stop sinning. The more the Holy Spirit teaches us about the sin that is within us, the more we will stand amazed at Jesus' love and mercy. He knew how completely we had turned our backs on God, and yet he chose to die for us anyway. Jesus is looking for servants who recognize their sins and limitations, and yet who love him so deeply that they don't ever want to offend him or lead his people astray. He wants servants who turn from sin by turning to Jesus in repentance and trust.

The closer we come to Jesus, the humbler we become. And, the humbler we become, the more he can entrust us with his work. It is really a privilege to serve such a wonderful God. Let's bind ourselves closer to him and allow his love to keep us humble and simple.

"Jesus, we believe that you are the Savior of the world. Help us to turn from sin and to turn toward you today so that we can become the people you want us to be."

Mark 9:49—10:1

[49] "For every one will be salted with fire. [50] Salt is good; but if the salt has lost its saltness, how will you season it? Have salt in yourselves, and be at peace with one another."

[1] And he left there and went to the region of Judea and

beyond the Jordan, and crowds gathered to him again; and again, as his custom was, he taught them. 🔳🔳

Salt was a valued commodity in ancient times. One of its many uses by the Israelites was to place it in offerings for purification rites. The book of Leviticus instructed the Hebrews to put salt with all of their grain offerings (Leviticus 2:13). The prophet Elisha purified foul water by adding salt to it (2 Kings 2:19-20). Newborn babies were rubbed with salt (Ezekiel 16:4).

Salt also functions as a preservative, something that was especially important to people living in a hot, dry climate without the benefit of refrigeration. The Old Testament referred to a "covenant of salt" that the Lord made with the people of Israel as a permanent condition (Numbers 18:19). Thus, salt, the preservative, signified the everlasting contract between the Lord and his people.

When Jesus told his disciples that everyone would be "salted" with fire, he had just finished warning them that sin was such an obstacle to entering into the kingdom of God that it would be better to lose part of their body than to let sin remain (Mark 9:42-48). Jesus' promise of purification through salt and fire was fulfilled in his death on the cross, for his blood cleansed us of sin for all time.

"Salt is good" (Mark 9:50), Jesus reminded his followers, but when it loses its very essence—its "saltness"— it becomes useless. When we live as God's own people, living within his everlasting covenant, we become authentically human—restored from the fall of our first parents. As we grow closer to the Lord, we become more and more a part of him—we are "seasoned" with his salt.

This seasoning makes us attractive to others because as Christ lives within us, we reflect his nature. We can be Christ to our brothers and sisters.

"Have salt in yourselves, and be at peace with one another," Jesus concluded (Mark 9:50). God's own nature, transforming us, will help us to live in harmony with our spouses, our children, our parents, our neighbors, our friends. The Lord has called us to be "the salt of the earth" (Matthew 5:13), to stand out from the crowd by reflecting his glory. Let us be open to God's "salt," which will purify us and keep us in his grace.

"Father, we want to become your people, faithful to the covenant you made with us. Open us to your grace, that we may become Christ to others."

Mark 10:2-16

[2] And Pharisees came up and in order to test him asked, "Is it lawful for a man to divorce his wife?" [3] He answered them, "What did Moses command you?" [4] They said, "Moses allowed a man to write a certificate of divorce, and to put her away." [5] But Jesus said to them, "For your hardness of heart he wrote you this commandment. [6] But from the beginning of creation, 'God made them male and female.' [7] 'For this reason a man shall leave his father and mother and be joined to his wife, [8] and the two shall become one.' So they are no longer two but one. [9] What therefore God has joined together, let not man put asunder."
[10] And in the house the disciples asked him again about this matter. [11] And he said to them, "Whoever divorces his wife and

marries another, commits adultery against her; [12] and if she divorces her husband and marries another, she commits adultery."

[13] And they were bringing children to him, that he might touch them; and the disciples rebuked them. [14] But when Jesus saw it he was indignant, and said to them, "Let the children come to me, do not hinder them; for to such belongs the kingdom of God. [15] Truly, I say to you, whoever does not receive the kingdom of God like a child shall not enter it." [16] And he took them in his arms and blessed them, laying his hands upon them.

The Pharisees' question on marriage was not just an innocent inquiry posed by a group of perplexed believers. Rather, as they did throughout Jesus' ministry, the Pharisees were looking for a way to trap Jesus in his own words. Although formulated as if a simple "yes" or "no" would suffice, their question involved complex interpretations of Hebrew law. In addition, if he answered one way, he could be accused of disavowing John the Baptist's reproach of Herod for divorcing his wife and marrying his sister-in-law. If he agreed with John, however, he could become a target for Herod's anger.

Jesus did not allow himself to become enmeshed in the trap. Instead, he sought to raise the discussion to a higher level and take advantage of the opportunity to speak yet again of the Father's desire to unite us in love. By trying to trick Jesus with thorny legislative questions, the Pharisees had missed the whole point about God's plan for human marriage.

Jesus took his questioners back to the beginning, when God created man and woman in his own image and likeness and established that in marriage the two would become one flesh (Genesis 2:24). Jesus revealed marriage as a wonderful gift from God that is meant to reflect the union he longs to have with his people. Both kinds of union—between man and woman, and between God and his people—are meant to be so intimate that they must not be broken by anyone. What a privilege it is to be united intimately with God and another person!

As we consider the state of marriage in the world, perhaps even our own marriage, we may be tempted to look only at the difficulties and forget God's power and love. Let us pray for all marriages today, that they be protected and raised up to become wonderful signs of God's love for his people everywhere.

"Father, how grateful we are for your love. Fill our hearts with a deeper love for you. May your love for us overflow to others, to bring healing and reconciliation."

Mark 10:17-27

[17] And as he was setting out on his journey, a man ran up and knelt before him, and asked him, "Good Teacher, what must I do to inherit eternal life?" [18] And Jesus said to him, "Why do you call me good? No one is good but God alone. [19] You know the commandments: 'Do not kill, Do not commit adultery, Do not steal, Do not bear false witness, Do not defraud, Honor your father and mother.' " [20] And he said to him, "Teacher, all these I have observed from my youth."

[21] And Jesus looking upon him loved him, and said to him, "You lack one thing; go, sell what you have, and give to the poor, and you will have treasure in heaven; and come, follow me." [22] At that saying his countenance fell, and he went away sorrowful; for he had great possessions.

[23] And Jesus looked around and said to his disciples, "How hard it will be for those who have riches to enter the kingdom of God!" [24] And the disciples were amazed at his words. But Jesus said to them again, "Children, how hard it is for those who trust in riches to enter the kingdom of God! [25] It is easier for a camel to go through the eye of a needle than for a rich man to enter the kingdom of God." [26] And they were exceedingly astonished, and said to him, "Then who can be saved?"

[27] Jesus looked at them and said, "With men it is im-possible, but not with God; for all things are possible with God." 🔳🔳

All things are possible with God. (Mark 10:27)

The rich young man wanted the best of both worlds—the fullness of eternal life and worldly riches as well. Many of us also seek eternal life, but would we be willing to sell our house, car, clothes, and valuables and give the proceeds to the poor in order to depend on Christ for our personal fulfillment, shelter, food, and clothing? This may be impossible by human resolve, but Jesus tells us it is possible with God.

Jesus warned his disciples about the danger of riches: "It is easier for a camel to go through the eye of a needle than for a rich man to enter the kingdom of God" (Mark 10:25). The disciples were shocked. According to Judaic thought, wealth was attributed to divine favor; why should they have to give it up? It's no wonder they thought that Jesus was demanding too much of a successful young man who had so eagerly and faithfully obeyed the commandments.

Jesus loved this man's sincere desire and efforts to live out the commandments (Mark 10:21), so he invited him to become his disciple. He called him to place his wholehearted trust and dependence on God, as a child would look to its parents for everything. Jesus knew that the priceless pearl of eternal life was worth selling everything to obtain (Matthew 13:45-46), but the rich young man could not yet see the pearl's incomparable value, and so he could not relinquish his foothold in this world.

Jesus' call to discipleship is costly. He asks all of his followers to sacrifice everything for his sake. The reward, though, is great; as we trust in him, he will enable us to place our security in the kingdom of God and so obtain eternal life. We may wonder if this is possible. Jesus assures us, "With men it is impossible, but not with God; for all things are possible with God" (Mark 10:27). Christ has accomplished the impossible for us through his perfect dependence and trust in the Father as he gave his life for us on the cross.

"Heavenly Father, for whom all things are possible, help us to devote our entire lives to Jesus with the trust and dependence of little children so that we may share eternal life with you."

Mark 10:28-31

²⁸ Peter began to say to him, "Lo, we have left everything and followed you." ²⁹ Jesus said, "Truly, I say to you, there is no one who has left house or brothers or sisters or mother or father or children or lands, for my sake and for the gospel, ³⁰ who will not receive a hundredfold now in this time, houses and brothers and sisters and mothers and children and lands, with persecutions, and in the age to come eternal life. ³¹ But many that are first will be last, and the last first."

We have left everything and followed you. (Mark 10:28)

How typical of Peter, the impetuous fisherman who always spoke his mind bluntly! You can just imagine him spluttering: "What will there be for us? How do we know we won't be left empty-handed?" Peter's concern was valid. If you give up everything for the kingdom, you are left—quite literally—with nothing. You become one of the poor—an outcast—considered weak and ineffectual. No wonder the rich man went away sad: Everything that had been his security was shown to be a distraction and burden.

Because Peter's question was valid, Jesus answered him directly, promising that the last would ultimately become the first (Mark 10:31). Jesus' own life shows the great reversal that all his disciples will experience: The Son who emptied himself to death on a cross would be exalted to the highest place (Philippians 2:6-11). This great promise is the glory and hope of all who embrace the gospel.

It is also wonderful encouragement for all of us who are on the road of discipleship and cannot quite see the light at the end.

Dietrich Bonhoeffer, a German Lutheran pastor who was executed in the closing days of World War II for his opposition to Adolf Hitler, also knew the cost of discipleship and the hope held out for those who leave everything to follow Christ. While he sought to give up everything for the sake of the kingdom, Bonhoeffer kept the Lord's promise close to his heart:

> Jesus is here speaking to men who have become individuals for his sake, who have left all at his call. . . .They receive the promise of a new fellowship. According to the word of Jesus, they will receive in this time a hundredfold of what they have left. Jesus is referring to his Church, which finds itself in him. He who leaves his father for Jesus' sake does most assuredly find father and mother, brothers and sisters again, and even lands and houses. Though we all have to enter upon discipleship alone, we do not remain alone. If we take him at his word and dare to become individuals, our reward is the fellowship of the Church. Here is a visible brotherhood to compensate a hundredfold for all we have lost. (*The Cost of Discipleship*, p. 113)

"Lord, help us to know your love to such an extent that we would willingly leave everything to follow you. Grant us the gift of fellowship with each other as we place all our hope and trust in you."

Mark 10:32-45

[32] And they were on the road, going up to Jerusalem, and Jesus was walking ahead of them; and they were amazed, and those who followed were afraid. And taking the twelve again, he began to tell them what was to happen to him, [33] saying, "Behold, we are going up to Jerusalem; and the Son of man will be delivered to the chief priests and the scribes, and they will condemn him to death, and deliver him to the Gentiles; [34] and they will mock him, and spit upon him, and scourge him, and kill him; and after three days he will rise."

[35] And James and John, the sons of Zebedee, came forward to him, and said to him, "Teacher, we want you to do for us whatever we ask of you." [36] And he said to them, "What do you want me to do for you?" [37] And they said to him, "Grant us to sit, one at your right hand and one at your left, in your glory." [38] But Jesus said to them, "You do not know what you are asking. Are you able to drink the cup that I drink, or to be baptized with the baptism with which I am baptized?" [39] And they said to him, "We are able." And Jesus said to them, "The cup that I drink you will drink; and with the baptism with which I am baptized, you will be baptized; [40] but to sit at my right hand or at my left is not mine to grant, but it is for those for whom it has been prepared."

[41] And when the ten heard it, they began to be indignant at James and John. [42] And Jesus called them to him and said to them, "You know that those who are supposed to rule over the Gentiles lord it over them, and their great men exercise authority over them. [43] But it shall not be so among you; but whoever would be great among you must be your servant, [44] and whoever would be first among you must be slave of all. [45] For the Son of man also came not to be served but to serve, and to give his life as a ransom for many."

When James and John asked Jesus for places of honor in his kingdom, Jesus took the opportunity to teach his disciples that to be great in the kingdom of God, they must become servants—just like him. He knew that in his Father's eyes, it was the servants who would receive high positions, not the highly honored (Mark 10:43-44). Throughout his life, Jesus was consumed by a love that compelled him to live for others, never for himself. In Jesus' eyes, this is what it meant to be a king—to lay down his life for his friends.

Jesus offered James and John the privilege of sharing in his sufferings, but this did not mean that their sufferings would take away people's sins. Only Jesus could redeem the whole world by his death and resurrection. No other sacrifice was needed. Still, he offered them the privilege of bearing his burdens as well as his joy and so becoming as compassionate as he was.

When we return love for hatred, when we are misunderstood and spoken against, when we sacrifice our time and energy to perform thankless, hidden acts of love, we share in Jesus' suffering. What could cause more pain than to love so deeply, and not be loved in return? Yet it was Jesus' very act of self-giving that was so pleasing to God, precisely because it did not seek reward, but sought only the blessing of those he loved.

In our own ways, each of us is called to drink from Jesus' cup. Who among us does not face opportunities every day to lay down our lives for others? Who does not sense the call to draw closer to the Lord by giving up our lives—even in the smallest of ways—for our friends? By our willingness to serve, we can reflect the life and love of Jesus, the humblest of servants. What a privilege, to share in Jesus' sufferings that we may also share in his glory!

"Father, we want to say yes to you and drink the cup that you offer us today. Make us like Jesus, who came not to be served, but to serve. Holy Spirit, fill us with your love, that we might love you and joyfully serve your people."

Mark 10:46-52

46 And they came to Jericho; and as he was leaving Jericho with his disciples and a great multitude, Bartimaeus, a blind beggar, the son of Timaeus, was sitting by the roadside. 47 And when he heard that it was Jesus of Nazareth, he began to cry out and say, "Jesus, Son of David, have mercy on me!" 48 And many rebuked him, telling him to be silent; but he cried out all the more, "Son of David, have mercy on me!" 49 And Jesus stopped and said, "Call him." And they called the blind man, saying to him, "Take heart; rise, he is calling you." 50 And throwing off his mantle he sprang up and came to Jesus. 51 And Jesus said to him, "What do you want me to do for you?" And the blind man said to him, "Master, let me receive my sight." 52 And Jesus said to him, "Go your way; your faith has made you well." And immediately he received his sight and followed him on the way.

The healing of Bartimaeus occurs, in the structure of Mark's Gospel, in the section recounting Jesus' journey to Jerusalem. The context is important to keep in mind. Bartimaeus' healing was the last reported incident prior to Jesus' entry into the city. There, he would suffer his passion, lay down his life, and take it up again. There, he would complete his ministry on earth. Just before the final act of this drama, in which Jesus accomplished the mission set by his Father, we have an account of a miracle. Like all of Jesus' miracles, it is a sign that the Messiah is present. It is a sign that God saves his people.

Jeremiah had prophesied that the blind and the lame would be among the remnant of Israel who would return with consolation from exile in Babylon. The consolation would be the sign proving that the Lord saves his people (Jeremiah 31:7-9). " 'The LORD has done great things for them.' The LORD has done great things for us" (Psalm 126:2-3).

In the divine plan of salvation, God takes the first step; it is he who saves. We respond. That was true for the exiles whom he freed from Babylon; it was true for the blind man whom Jesus healed; it is true for us. The response is not unimportant, but it is not self-generated either. Faith is a gift of God. It was Bartimaeus' faith that led him to cry out to Jesus, to persist in the face of opposition, and come to Jesus when called. His faith opened him up to the work of Jesus in him, and that is an important message for us as well.

As we see the work of Jesus in Bartimaeus and in our own lives, we must remember that the healing we see is not an end or goal in itself. Rather, it is a sign of the new world that emerged from the coming of Jesus and his passion, death, and resurrection, a new world that we will know in fullness when Jesus comes again. Jesus is the door to a whole new existence for us, as he was for Bartimaeus. As great as it was for Bartimaeus to be able to see, he knew this was a sign, a call from Jesus, and he "followed him on the way" (Mark 10:52). As great as any healing is, it should be seen as a call into the new existence that Christ has won for us.

A D E V O T I O N A L C O M M E N T A R Y O N M A R K

Conflicts in Jerusalem

MARK
11–12

Mark 11:1-10

[1] And when they drew near to Jerusalem, to Bethphage and Bethany, at the Mount of Olives, he sent two of his disciples, [2] and said to them, "Go into the village opposite you, and immediately as you enter it you will find a colt tied, on which no one has ever sat; untie it and bring it. [3] If any one says to you, 'Why are you doing this?' say, 'The Lord has need of it and will send it back here immediately.' " [4] And they went away, and found a colt tied at the door out in the open street; and they untied it. [5] And those who stood there said to them, "What are you doing, untying the colt?" [6] And they told them what Jesus had said; and they let them go. [7] And they brought the colt to Jesus, and threw their garments on it; and he sat upon it. [8] And many spread their garments on the road, and others spread leafy branches which they had cut from the fields. [9] And those who went before and those who followed cried out, "Hosanna! Blessed is he who comes in the name of the Lord! [10] Blessed is the kingdom of our father David that is coming! Hosanna in the highest!"

I f there was any moment of earthly glory for Jesus, this was it. The people of Jerusalem were more than just curious to see in person this prophet they had heard so much about. They were ready to pay him homage, to proclaim him the long-awaited Messiah. The prophet Zechariah had prophesied that the Israel's king would enter Jersualem "triumphant and victorious . . . humble and riding on an ass" (Zechariah 9:9). For this moment, at least, the people recognized their true king, though his outward appearance did not in any way resemble royalty.

Jesus knew all too well that these enthusiastic greetings would soon become cries for his execution. "The light has come into the world, and men loved darkness rather than light" (John 3:19). The people had seen a great light but many, especially the religious leaders, preferred the darkness. The light of Jesus was too blinding. It cast a searchlight on their hypocrisy and their sinfulness. Rather than humbling themselves and repenting, they chose to extinguish the light.

The light of Jesus, however, can never be extinguished. Destroying death, he shone with glory in the Resurrection and won for us eternal life. Now his light shines in every corner of the earth. He enters our hearts as he entered Jerusalem on that day 2,000 years ago, in humility and poverty. He is not a king who gains victory by force. He only knocks, and waits for us to open the door. If we open our hearts, our lives will be changed. The brilliance of his love will root out sin. He will ask us to walk the path he walked, a humble path that leads to the death of our own selfish desires and to our loving others with the sacrificial love of Jesus.

Like Jesus, we will rarely hear the cheers of the crowd as we walk the narrow road to eternal life. Mostly, our lives will be defined by small acts of love for one another. Yet because Christ lives in us, our inner light will shine. Sometimes others will notice. We can tell them that we have let the King of kings into our hearts, and though he found the house disorderly and unclean, he decided to stay. He never refuses anyone who asks him to enter.

"Lord Jesus, you reign in our hearts forever. May your light dissolve any darkness in our lives."

Mark 11:11-26

[11] And he entered Jerusalem, and went into the temple; and when he had looked round at everything, as it was already late, he went out to Bethany with the twelve.
[12] On the following day, when they came from Bethany, he was hungry. [13] And seeing in the distance a fig tree in leaf, he went to see if he could find anything on it. When he came to it, he found nothing but leaves, for it was not the season for figs. [14] And he said to it, "May no one ever eat fruit from you again." And his disciples heard it.
[15] And they came to Jerusalem. And he entered the temple and began to drive out those who sold and those who bought in the temple, and he overturned the tables of the money-changers and the seats of those who sold pigeons; [16] and he would not allow any one to carry anything through the temple. [17] And he taught, and said to them, "Is it not written, 'My house shall be called a house of prayer for all the nations? But you have made it a den of robbers." [18] And the chief priests and the scribes heard it and sought a way to destroy him; for they feared him, because all the multitude was astonished at his teaching. [19] And when evening came they went out of the city.
[20] As they passed by in the morning, they saw the fig tree withered away to its roots. [21] And Peter remembered and said to him, "Master, look! The fig tree which you cursed has withered." [22] And Jesus answered them, "Have faith in God. [23] Truly, I say to you, whoever says to this mountain, 'Be taken up and cast into the sea,' and does not doubt in his heart, but believes that what he says will come to pass, it will be done for him. [24] Therefore I tell you, whatever you ask in prayer, believe that you receive it, and you will. [25] And whenever you stand praying, forgive, if you have anything against any one; so that your Father also who is in heaven may forgive you your trespasses."

Jesus' cursing of the fig tree has always been a difficult text for Bible commentators, especially in view of Mark's comment that "it was not the season for figs" (Mark 11:13). It seems odd that Jesus would curse the fig tree when it was not the time for it to bear fruit.

Some commentators link this passage with segments from other prophetic works (Jeremiah 8:13; Hosea 9:10; Joel 1:7) to suggest that the fig tree represents the barrenness of the Pharisees' legalism, which was prevalent in Israel at that time. Earlier in his gospel (Mark 7:1-8), Mark had noted how the Pharisees complained that the disciples did not observe their legalistic practices. Jesus—at that time—condemned their hypocrisy and legalism.

After cursing the fig tree, Jesus moved on to take possession of the temple, where prevailing attitudes and practices had turned God's house into a "den of robbers" (probably quoting from Jeremiah 7:11). On their return from the temple, Peter was surprised to see that the fig tree had withered (Mark 11:20). Jesus used this occasion to give a teaching about the need for faith, the power of prayer, and the need for repentance (11:22-25).

Faith, prayer, and repentance; these are the fruits of Jesus' teaching. By contrast, the teaching of the Pharisees—that a rigid observance of Jewish law and tradition was what mattered—resulted in a barren spirituality that withered away.

The barrenness condemned by Jesus can cause us problems as well. We are called to bear fruit; Jesus wants that fruit. If we are willing to be satisfied with legalistic observances, we will remain barren. We can never plead that it is not the proper season to bear fruit, that we have no time for prayer, no need for repentance, no reason for faith. We can argue that we go to church on Sunday, that people call us Christians, that we observe certain religious rituals. God, however, wants faith that bears fruit.

"Lord Jesus, as I gaze at your cross, I cannot doubt your love for me. Yet I know that you require from me a response to that love. So often I do things by rote, content with a fruitless faith. Change my heart, Lord. Increase my faith and give me a desire for prayer so that I may bear the fruit you want from me."

Mark 11:27-33

27 And they came again to Jerusalem. And as he was walking in the temple, the chief priests and the scribes and the elders came to him, 28 and they said to him, "By what authority are you doing these things, or who gave you this authority to do them?" 29 Jesus said to them, "I will ask you a question; answer me, and I will tell you by what authority I do these things. 30 Was the baptism of John from heaven or from men? Answer me." 31 And they argued with one another, "If we say, 'From heaven,' he will say, 'Why then did you not believe him?' 32 But shall we say, 'From men'?"— they were afraid of the people, for all held that John was a real prophet. 33 So they answered Jesus, "We do not know." And Jesus said to them, "Neither will I tell you by what authority I do these things."

The chief priests, scribes, and elders must have been amazed by this man Jesus! On his way to Jerusalem, he had healed a blind man. As he entered the city, the people hailed him with the greeting: "Blessed is he who comes in the name of the Lord!" (Mark 11:9). Then he made a scene in the temple by over-turning the tables of the money-changers. Whatever their feelings about him, this was not a man who could be ignored!

The question posed to Jesus by the priests and elders about where he derived his authority was countered by a question to them: Where did John the Baptist get his authority? The question made the leaders uncomfortable. Although the people had discerned that John's authority came from God, the Jewish leaders were not ready to acknowledge this. John had led his people to repentance through baptism and prepared them for the coming of the Savior. But John, like Jesus, was not an ordained rabbi. The Jewish leaders, who were, after all, accountable for the spiritual welfare of their people, must have wondered why God would choose to work through itinerant, poverty-stricken preachers instead of through them.

The Greek root for the word "authority" connotes a divine commission. Jesus refused to answer the Jewish leaders because he knew that they would not believe him if he told them he had been commissioned by God to redeem the world. The very idea probably would have rankled them to the core. The truth would have meant a painful re-examination of themselves before God, a soul-searching experience they preferred to avoid. They chose, instead, to lose the argument with Jesus.

For all of us, the truth about ourselves can be difficult to face. When we realize how we have strayed and how we may have hurt others through our sinfulness, we can feel humiliated. But, as Jesus told the Jewish believers: "The truth will make you free" (John 8:32). The healing of our painful experiences is to be found in the joy and peace of true repentance and conversion, in the freedom that Jesus described. It was a path the Jewish leaders refused to take.

"Lord Jesus, you are the way, the truth, and the life. Help us to face the truth about ourselves so that we may experience the freedom you offer us through your cross and resurrection."

Mark 12:1-12

[1] And he began to speak to them in parables. "A man planted a vineyard, and set a hedge around it, and dug a pit for the wine press, and built a tower, and let it out to tenants, and went into another country. [2] When the time came, he sent a servant to the tenants, to get from them some of the fruit of the vineyard. [3] And they took him and beat him, and sent him away empty-handed. [4] Again he sent to them another servant, and they wounded him in the head, and treated him shamefully. [5] And he sent another, and him they killed; and so with many others, some they beat and some they killed. [6] He had still one other, a beloved son; finally he sent him to them, saying, 'They will respect my son.' [7] But those tenants said to one another, 'This is the heir; come, let us kill him, and the inheritance will be ours.' [8] And they took him and killed him, and cast him out of the vineyard. [9] What will the owner of the vineyard do? He will come and destroy the tenants, and give the vineyard to others. [10] Have you not read this scripture: 'The very stone which the builders rejected has become the head of the corner; [11] this was the Lord's doing, and it is marvelous in our eyes'?"

¹² And they tried to arrest him, but feared the
multitude, for they perceived that he had told the parable
against them; so they left him and went away.

In a stinging rebuke of the Jewish hierarchy, Jesus told a parable
that not only predicted his death at their hands, but also related
them to leaders in past generations who had killed the prophets.
He depicted Israel as a vineyard under the control of the Jewish
leaders—the wicked tenants. God was the owner, and the servants
he sent to gather the vineyard's harvest were the prophets. Jesus was
the owner's beloved son, whose murder at the hands of the tenants
prompted the owner to exact punishment.

At the end of the parable, Jesus quoted Psalm 118: "The very
stone which the builders rejected has become the head of the corner" (Mark 12:10; see Psalm 118:22)—an appropriate way to make
his point, for Jesus would become the head of the church. He went
on: "This was the Lord's doing, and it is marvelous in our eyes"
(Mark 12:11; see Psalm 118:23). This additional verse must have
seemed very much out of place, even inappropriate, to Jesus' audience. What could be so "marvelous" in this story?

This is where God's wisdom finds its full expression. Knowing
what awaited him there, Jesus insisted on going to Jerusalem. He
allowed himself to be convicted of crimes he did not commit. He
suffered a cruel and humiliating death, never once opening his
mouth in protest. He endured such treatment because he knew
that his death would reconcile us to the Father. Now risen in
glory, Jesus has poured out his Spirit, offering everyone a share in
his resurrection.

At times when we find ourselves in unfair or painful situations, perhaps through no fault of our own, we can turn to this parable—and Jesus' own experience in Jerusalem—for help. Whatever the situation, if we love God, we can be sure that he is at work, building a solid foundation of faith and trust in him (Romans 8:28). Just as the father allowed Jesus to suffer so that we might have a living relationship with him, so he uses events in our lives to form Jesus' character in us. God will ultimately bring justice and peace. We need only to entrust our lives to him.

"Father, we surrender all our situations to you and thank you for your wisdom in every circumstance. Holy Spirit, enable us to embrace your calling with confidence. Open our eyes to see the greater good that you are doing in our hearts."

Mark 12:13-17

[13] And they sent to him some of the Pharisees and some of the Herodians, to entrap him in his talk. [14] And they came and said to him, "Teacher, we know that you are true, and care for no man; for you do not regard the position of men, but truly teach the way of God. Is it lawful to pay taxes to Caesar, or not? [15] Should we pay them, or should we not?" But knowing their hypocrisy, he said to them, "Why put me to the test? Bring me a coin, and let me look at it." [16] And they brought one. And he said to them, "Whose likeness and inscription is this?" They said to him, "Caesar's." [17] Jesus said to them, "Render to Caesar the things that are Caesar's, and to God the things that are God's." And they were amazed at him.

The days following Jesus' triumphant entry into Jerusalem had grown increasingly tense. After witnessing his display of righteous anger in the temple, the chief priests and scribes began plotting against Jesus (Mark 11:15-19). In another calculated attempt to ensnare Jesus by his own words, the chief priests enlisted the help of some Pharisees and supporters of King Herod.

After first complimenting Jesus, they asked him whether the Jews should pay the Roman poll tax—a tax that constantly reminded the Jews of their subordination to Rome. The trap was set. If Jesus answered that the tax should be paid, the Pharisees (who were Jewish nationalists) would reject him as a collaborator with Rome. If he said it should not be paid, the Herodians would report Jesus as a dangerous revolutionary.

Recognizing the trap, however, Jesus raised the question from the political plane to the spiritual. According to Jesus, the Roman coins had Caesar's image stamped on them, and so they belonged to Caesar. Likewise, every human heart has God's image engraved on it, and so we belong to God. By answering their question in this way, Jesus wasn't trying to just put the Pharisees and Herodians in their place; he sought to give them a bigger picture of who we all are and what we can become. It was no longer an issue of which laws should be obeyed. The real issue was whether God was able to transform the human heart to resemble his own heart of mercy, compassion, and love.

God has stamped his image upon each of our hearts. We belong to him in a very deep and intimate way, and his image can shine out of us and touch others with the love of our heavenly Father. As we turn to Jesus in prayer, we can ask the Holy Spirit to empower us to love as Jesus loved us, to forgive as we have been forgiven, and to give to others as generously as God has given to us. Through the witness of our transformed lives, Jesus' image can be known in this world, bringing hope and relief to all who suffer.

"Father, you formed us and called us by name; we are yours. By your Spirit, conform us to Jesus' likeness so that your love may touch everyone we meet today."

Mark 12:18-27

[18] And Sadducees came to him, who say that there is no resurrection; and they asked him a question, saying, [19] "Teacher, Moses wrote for us that if a man's brother dies and leaves a wife, but leaves no child, the man must take the wife, and raise up children for his brother. [20] There were seven brothers; the first took a wife, and when he died left no children; [21] and the second took her, and died, leaving no children; and the third likewise; [22] and the seven left no children. Last of all the woman also died. [23] In the resurrection whose wife will she be? For the seven had her as wife."

[24] Jesus said to them, "Is not this why you are wrong, that you know neither the scriptures nor the power of God? [25] For when they rise from the dead, they neither marry nor are given in marriage, but are like angels in heaven. [26] And as for the dead being raised, have you not read in the book of Moses, in the passage about the bush, how God said to him, 'I am the God of Abraham, and the God of Isaac, and the God of Jacob'? [27] He is not God of the dead, but of the living; you are quite wrong."

The Sadducees were primarily wealthy, sophisticated Jews who made the temple and its administration their main interest. Though small in number, they exerted a powerful influence on the people. Because they accepted only the Pentateuch (the first five books of the Hebrew scripture) as authoritative, they flatly rejected the rabbinic oral tradition, which would have been more open to the possibility of a resurrection from the dead.

In this context, the Sadducees' puzzle about the much-married widow was both legalistic and cynical. Using an example taken from the book of Deuteronomy (25:5-10), they interpreted it in a way meant to reduce to absurdity any belief in the resurrection, and thus humiliate Jesus.

As with the Pharisees' previous attempt (Mark 12:13-17), however, the Sadducees' riddle became an occasion for Jesus to reveal the hope of the gospel. Meeting them on their own terms, he explained how the resurrection is foreshadowed even in the Pentateuch. God revealed himself to Moses as the God of his ancestors (Exodus 3:6,15-16), and yet also as a God who is still alive and active. Jesus explained that even the Pentateuch speaks of the hope of resurrection, and this hope rests upon the character of God, who graciously overcomes death and gives life to his people, no matter how dire their condition.

By looking only to the Pentateuch for authentic teaching, the Sadducees created an intellectual and spiritual elitism that blinded them to the full spectrum of God's ways. Perceiving their arrogance and self-confidence, Jesus sought to show them that God is too big and his word is too expansive for anyone to believe that he or she can understand it all. Throughout his entire ministry, in fact, Jesus proved that God often moves in ways that seem new or unexpected to us because of our limited grasp of how wide and high and deep his love is. The resurrection is our greatest hope and joy, yet the Sadducees, with their limited view of God and his word, risked missing this wonderful promise.

"Father, you are the God of the living who sent your Son to ransom us from death. May we never seek to restrict you to the limitations of our minds. By your grace, draw us ever closer to Jesus, and through your word, continue to nourish us with the revelation of your wondrous plan for us."

Mark 12:28-34

[28] And one of the scribes came up and heard them disputing with one another, and seeing that he answered them well, asked him, "Which commandment is the first of all?" [29] Jesus answered, "The first is, 'Hear, O Israel: The Lord our God, the Lord is one; [30] and you shall love the Lord your God with all your heart, and with all your soul, and with all your mind, and with all your strength.' [31] The second is this, 'You shall love your neighbor as yourself.' There is no other commandment greater than these." [32] And the scribe said to him, "You are right, Teacher; you have truly said that he is one, and there is no other but he; [33] and to love him with all the heart, and with all the understanding, and with all the strength, and to love one's neighbor as oneself, is much more than all whole burnt offerings and sacrifices." [34] And when Jesus saw that he answered wisely, he said to him, "You are not far from the kingdom of God." And after that no one dared to ask him any question.

J ewish literature relates that a man once came to the famous Rabbi Hillel and asked him to sum up the 613 precepts of the Old Testament law while the man stood on one leg (in other words: briefly!). Hillel replied: "What you hate for yourself, do not do to your neighbor. This is the whole law; the rest is commentary."

Stepping out from the majority of the scribes and priests (who were bent on destroying Jesus), one scribe asked Jesus a similar question, but with remarkable honesty and sincerity: "Which commandment is the first of all?" (Mark 12:28). While many of the other religious leaders saw Jesus as a threat, this man saw in him an opportunity to learn, and so he posed a simple question that expressed a concern embedded deep within every heart.

The scribe's desire to know the greatest commandment reflects a heart that was seeking to grasp, if possible, a single simple principle underlying the complexity of the law. What does God want of us? What foundational commandment can give meaning to all the smaller rules and regulations of religious life? Is there a key that can unlock the riddle of our lives and guide us through the complexity that is both around and within us? We all yearn for answers to these questions, and Jesus' response offers us a sure foundation and purpose.

The command to love God and neighbor is not just an order or duty. After all, no one can love simply because he is told to do so! We must also align our wills with this greatest of commandments, making the decision to ask God to teach us how to love and obey him. Ultimately, loving God is a privilege, a relationship that God initiates at our baptism and that grows as we accept God's words and open our hearts to experience his love.

God is always reaching out to us, and every time we turn to him, we can receive his love more deeply. As a result, we are then moved to love him and to share this love with others. It is true that we have to decide to seek God and respond to him, but these decisions are meant to flow from the loving relationship that grows as love is shared.

"Heavenly Father, move us by your love to love you and love others with your love. Help us to see our life of faith as a relationship, not just a duty."

Mark 12:35-37

³⁵ And as Jesus taught in the temple, he said, "How can the scribes say that the Christ is the son of David? ³⁶ David himself, inspired by the Holy Spirit, declared, 'The Lord said to my Lord, Sit at my right hand, till I put thy enemies under thy feet.' ³⁷ David himself calls him Lord; so how is he his son?" And the great throng heard him gladly.

There must have been something in Jesus' words to move the people not just to listen to him, but to listen "gladly" (Mark 12:37). What would have delighted them so much? In these few words, Jesus showed his listeners that their long-awaited Messiah would be higher and grander than anything they had imagined. For centuries, the term messiah (or "anointed one") had been applied to certain select members of God's people: first Israel's kings, and then the high priest. Yet in the very temple where the high priest would offer sacrifices, in the very city where David reigned, Jesus told the people that the Messiah, the fulfillment of all their hopes, would not simply be a man like the kings and priests they knew. He would be more.

Quoting Psalm 110:1 in which David showed deference not only to God ("the Lord"), but also to another person who knows an intimate relationship with God ("my Lord"), Jesus showed that David anticipated one who was even greater than himself. He would be "Lord," with the authority and power of God. He would not simply be the anointed Messiah of Israel; he would be sovereign over all peoples. His kingdom would far surpass David's, both in scope and in depth, for not only would he rule over all people; he would reign in unending peace and justice. The ancient enemies of sin and death would no longer hold sway, and the righteousness and love of God would become the law of the land.

We who live after the resurrection of Christ know that Jesus is this promised Messiah and Lord. By his cross, he has overcome all our enemies and inaugurated the kingdom of heaven. He is the anointed one on whom the Spirit of the Lord rests (Isaiah 61:1-2; Luke 4:16-21) and, in him we too are anointed with the Spirit and made into a "royal priesthood, a holy nation, God's own people" (1 Peter 2:9). In prayer today, let us ask the Spirit to reveal Jesus to us as our Messiah and Lord. It is his greatest desire to open up for us the riches of the knowledge of Christ (Colossians 2:2), and it is our heritage as sons and daughters of God.

"Holy Spirit, fill our hearts today with the knowledge of Jesus. Let us see him as David saw him, and move us to delight in him, our great Messiah and Lord."

Mark 12:38-44

[38] And in his teaching he said, "Beware of the scribes, who like to go about in long robes, and to have salutations in the market places [39] and the best seats in the synagogues and the places of honor at feasts, [40] who devour widows' houses and for a pretense make long prayers. They will receive the greater condemnation."

[41] And he sat down opposite the treasury, and watched the multitude putting money into the treasury. Many rich people put in large sums. [42]And a poor widow came, and put in two copper coins, which make a penny. [43] And he called his disciples to him, and said to them, "Truly, I say to you, this poor widow has put in more than all those who are contributing to the treasury. [44] For they all contributed out of their abundance; but she out of her poverty has put in everything she had, her whole living."

The story of the widow's mite demonstrates powerfully the humility and lowliness that so pleases Jesus. We can tend to think that being humble means allowing other people to take advantage of us, but this widow demonstrated that true humility means radical dependence on God.

The widow's humility is even more remarkable when she is compared with those who put "large sums" into the temple treasury (Mark 12:41). Many of these donors were probably giving the amount dictated by the law, yet it was still money they could spare. Consequently, they could go away satisfied with their contribution but failing to grasp how God wanted them to depend on him for everything. In contrast, the widow's donation was only the smallest of coins, but it was "her whole living" (12:44).

It is significant that Mark placed this story before Jesus' description of the final judgment (Mark 13:1-37). When the Lord returns, will he find a people who are humble and needy, willing to surrender their lives totally to him? Or will he find a people full of pride and arrogance, who have no room for him in their hearts? The widow had the faith to believe that even if she gave God everything she had to live on, he would never let her down. He was worth everything she had, and she willingly placed herself in his hands.

Today in prayer, let us ask the Lord to make us more like this poor widow. Perhaps he will lead us to pray more often during the day, or to spend more time reading his word or praying with our families. The Holy Spirit may also reveal sin in our hearts that we never knew was there—and give us the grace to repent and be free. There are so many ways that humility and dependence on God can open the door to a deeper relationship with him. Jesus himself promised us: "Blessed are the poor in spirit, for theirs is the kingdom of heaven" (Matthew 5:3).

"Heavenly Father, we come to you with humble hearts, knowing that you alone can fill our every need. Heal us and forgive us for the ways that we turn from your presence and choose self-reliance over dependence on you. Pour out your love and mercy on us as we joyfully await your return in glory."

On the End Times

MARK
13

Mark 13:1-23

¹ And as he came out of the temple, one of his disciples said to him, "Look, Teacher, what wonderful stones and what wonderful buildings! ² And Jesus said to him, "Do you see these great buildings? There will not be left here one stone upon another, that will not be thrown down."

³ And as he sat on the Mount of Olives opposite the temple, Peter and James and John and Andrew asked him privately, ⁴ "Tell us, when will this be, and what will be the sign when these things are all to be accomplished?" ⁵ And Jesus began to say to them, "Take heed that no one leads you astray. ⁶ Many will come in my name, saying, 'I am he!' and they will lead many astray. ⁷ And when you hear of wars and rumors of wars, do not be alarmed; this must take place, but the end is not yet. ⁸ For nation will rise against nation, and kingdom against kingdom; there will be earthquakes in various places, there will be famines; this is but the beginning of the sufferings.

⁹ "But take heed to yourselves; for they will deliver you up to councils; and you will be beaten in synagogues; and you will stand before governors and kings for my sake, to bear testimony before them. ¹⁰ And the gospel must first be preached to all nations. ¹¹ And when they bring you to trial and deliver you up, do not be anxious beforehand what you are to say; but say whatever is given you in that hour, for it is not you who speak, but the Holy Spirit. ¹² And brother will deliver up brother to death, and the father his child, and children will rise against parents and have them put to death; ¹³ and you will be hated by all for my name's sake. But he who endures to the end will be saved.

¹⁴ "But when you see the desolating sacrilege set up where it ought not to be (let the reader understand), then let those who are in Judea flee to the mountains; ¹⁵ let him who is on the

housetop not go down, nor enter his house, to take anything away; [16] and let him who is in the field not turn back to take his mantle. [17] And alas for those who are with child and for those who give suck in those days! [18] Pray that it may not happen in winter. [19] For in those days there will be such tribulation as has not been from the beginning of the creation which God created until now, and never will be. [20] And if the Lord had not shortened the days, no human being would be saved; but for the sake of the elect, whom he chose, he shortened the days. [21] And then if any one says to you, 'Look, here is the Christ!' or 'Look, there he is!' do not believe it. [22] False Christs and false prophets will arise and show signs and wonders, to lead astray, if possible, the elect. [23] But take heed; I have told you all things beforehand. ▓▓▓

A simple observation by one of Jesus' disciples about the beauty of the temple led Jesus to speak prophetically about a terrible future event. The "wonderful stones and . . . wonderful buildings" (Mark 13:1) would someday be destroyed. The early Christians knew the truth of Jesus' words only too well, for Jerusalem and its magnificent temple were destroyed in 70 A.D.

The disciples, however, wanted to know the specifics: "When will this be, and what will be the sign when these things are all to be accomplished?" (Mark 13:4). Jesus told them of signs: Wars, earthquakes, and famines. The disciples would be persecuted for spreading the gospel, and families would fight among themselves. Despite all this tribulation, however, Jesus assured his followers that God would save the elect: "But he who endures to the end will be saved" (Mark 13:13). Jesus did not ask us to endure on our own, however. Even as he described the persecution his disciples would undergo, he also exhorted them not to be anxious (Mark 13:11). The Holy Spirit would speak through them, answering the charges brought against them.

Whether or not we live to experience the "end times" described by Jesus, we will be faced with trials in our lives. But we can take comfort in Jesus' reassuring words. If we are God's chosen people—if we in fact choose to live our lives for the Lord—he will protect us. In the end, we will be saved. Someday—we do not know when—all of God's faithful will be resurrected in glory, to live in the new heaven and new earth (Revelation 21:1)

As we journey along the way, we should never hesitate to cry out to Jesus when we are in need. He who has promised to care for us even through the worst tribulations the world has ever known will see us through our own difficulties. He will not abandon those who have asked him into their hearts. There he will reside, experiencing both our sorrows and our joys. We have nothing to fear with Jesus by our side.

"Father, give us the courage to face each day, and the faith to believe that you will never leave us. We know how much you desire to save us. We long for the day when we will see you face to face. Help us to be always ready for your Son's return in glory."

Mark 13:24-32

24 "But in those days, after that tribulation, the sun will be darkened, and the moon will not give its light, 25 and the stars will be falling from heaven, and the powers in the heavens will be shaken. 26 And then they will see the Son of man coming in clouds with great power and glory. 27 And then he will send out the angels, and gather his elect from the four winds, from the ends of the earth to the ends of heaven.
28 "From the fig tree learn its lesson: as soon as its branch becomes tender and puts forth its leaves, you know that summer is near. 29 So also, when you see these things taking place, you know that he is near, at the very gates. 30 Truly, I say to you, this generation will not pass away before all these things take place. 31 Heaven and earth will pass away, but my words will not pass away.
32 "But of that day or that hour no one knows, not even the angels in heaven, nor the Son, but only the Father. ▨▨▨

St. Lawrence Justinian (1381-1456) lay on his deathbed and said, "Until this hour all was child's play, but now comes the serious moment for the bridegroom is approaching and I must go forth to meet him." He raised his eyes to heaven, his face beaming with heavenly light, and cried out fervently, "I am coming sweetest Jesus. This day I have always kept before my mind. Thou knowest it, O Lord."

Whether we meet Jesus at our physical deaths (like Lawrence Justinian) or at the second coming, whichever comes first, we on earth are awaiting Jesus to take us to the heavenly kingdom. Like the ten virgins, our lamps are in our hands; we have been infused with the oil of grace and God's Holy Spirit dwells within us (Matthew 25:1-13). Jesus said that the day would surely come, but that only the Father in heaven would know the day and hour (Mark 13:32). In the meantime, Jesus knew his followers would have to endure trying times. He knew that deceivers would come and try to lure them from God, or that they would be distracted with their own cares and pursuits.

That is why the Lord said, "Take heed" (Mark 13:23). Scripture uses this mode of expression to exhort us to holy watchfulness and to serious preparation for the second coming (13:28-29). The Lord delays in order that all may come to repentance and true faith.

At the second coming, the angels in heaven will accompany their king to his court of justice. Their voices will resound like trumpets. The book of Daniel says: "At that time shall arise Michael, the great prince who has charge of your people. And there shall be a time of trouble . . . but at that time your people shall be delivered, every one whose name shall be found written in the book" (Daniel 12:1).

In the meantime, we must pray and remain alert. The devil will try to rob us of our peace or lull us into a false sense of security. "Preserve me, O God, for in you I take refuge. . . . You are my LORD. I have no good apart from you. . . . I keep the LORD always before me" (Psalm 16:1-2,8). You can be certain that all of God's promises will be fulfilled. We must trust the plan that God has for us and set our hearts on things above. We can be confident that if we die with him, we will also rise with him.

Mark 13:33-37

³³ Take heed, watch and pray; for you do not know when the time will come. ³⁴ It is like a man going on a journey, when he leaves home and puts his servants in charge, each with his work, and commands the doorkeeper to be on the watch. ³⁵ Watch therefore—for you do not know when the master of the house will come, in the evening, or at midnight, or at cockcrow, or in the morning—³⁶ lest he come suddenly and find you asleep. ³⁷ And what I say to you I say to all: Watch." ✵✵✵

Stay awake! Be alert! You don't know when the Master will come! The church calls all of her people to look with great anticipation toward the second coming of Jesus Christ, our Master, who wants to draw us close to his heart.

Throughout history, God has continually come to his people, at first in the promise of his word and his covenant, and then in the birth of his beloved Son. Jesus' purpose for entering into the world was to give his life for us on the cross. Now, raised to glory, he invites us to open our hearts to his Spirit and so be filled with lasting hope and joy for his second coming.

But what does all of this mean? First and foremost, it means that we are incredibly and dearly loved by our Father in heaven. God created us to be his people, to walk with him, and to be filled with his life and his love. After our first parents rejected God, he gave up his only Son in order to restore us to himself. Now, through Jesus, we have received the Holy Spirit who dwells in our hearts, enabling us to follow Christ. God's hand is always upon us.

He has prepared a place for us in heaven so that we can be with him for all eternity.

How different our lives would be if we knew more deeply God's love for us! We would experience the freedom to live in a way that draws us nearer to God; we would have a greater desire to do his will. Secure in our Father's love, we could go confidently to him to receive wisdom in day-to-day situations. Courage, hope, and strength would be ours in times of struggle as we experienced the safe haven of our Father's protection more deeply. We would love those around us with God's love inside of us; to love would not be a burden.

Let us prepare our hearts by welcoming Jesus into our lives as we begin each day. Let us ask him to open our eyes to enable us to see how close he is to us and how precious we are to him. Let us search the scriptures to see the innumerable reflections of his love for us. Every day we can know the joy of awaiting our Master's return.

A DEVOTIONAL COMMENTARY ON MARK

Jesus' Final Week

MARK
14–15

Mark 14:1-72

1   It was now two days before the Passover and the feast of Unleavened Bread. And the chief priests and the scribes were seeking how to arrest him by stealth, and kill him; 2 for they said, "Not during the feast, lest there be a tumult of the people."

3   And while he was at Bethany in the house of Simon the leper, as he sat at table, a woman came with an alabaster jar of ointment of pure nard, very costly, and she broke the jar and poured it over his head. 4 But there were some who said to themselves indignantly, "Why was the ointment thus wasted? 5 For this ointment might have been sold for more than three hundred denarii, and given to the poor." And they reproached her. 6 But Jesus said, "Let her alone; why do you trouble her? She has done a beautiful thing to me. 7 For you always have the poor with you, and whenever you will, you can do good to them; but you will not always have me. 8 She has done what she could; she has anointed my body beforehand for burying. 9 And truly, I say to you, wherever the gospel is preached in the whole world, what she has done will be told in memory of her."

10   Then Judas Iscariot, who was one of the twelve, went to the chief priests in order to betray him to them. 11 And when they heard it they were glad, and promised to give him money. And he sought an opportunity to betray him.

12   And on the first day of Unleavened Bread, when they sacrificed the passover lamb, his disciples said to him, "Where will you have us go and prepare for you to eat the passover?" 13 And he sent two of his disciples, and said to them, "Go into the city, and a man carrying a jar of water will meet you; follow him, 14 and wherever he enters, say to the householder, 'The Teacher says, Where is my guest room, where I am to eat the passover with my disciples?' 15 And he will show you a large upper room

furnished and ready; there prepare for us." [16] And the disciples set out and went to the city, and found it as he had told them; and they prepared the passover.
[17] And when it was evening he came with the twelve. [18] And as they were at table eating, Jesus said, "Truly, I say to you, one of you will betray me, one who is eating with me." [19] They began to be sorrowful, and to say to him one after another, "Is it I?" [20] He said to them, "It is one of the twelve, one who is dipping bread into the dish with me. [21] For the Son of man goes as it is written of him, but woe to that man by whom the Son of man is betrayed! It would have been better for that man if he had not been born."
[22] And as they were eating, he took bread, and blessed, and broke it, and gave it to them, and said, "Take; this is my body." [23] And he took a cup, and when he had given thanks he gave it to them, and they all drank of it. [24] And he said to them, "This is my blood of the covenant, which is poured out for many. [25] Truly, I say to you, I shall not drink again of the fruit of the vine until that day when I drink it new in the kingdom of God."
[26] And when they had sung a hymn, they went out to the Mount of Olives. [27] And Jesus said to them, "You will all fall away; for it is written, 'I will strike the shepherd, and the sheep will be scattered.' [28] But after I am raised up, I will go before you to Galilee." [29] Peter said to him, "Even though they all fall away, I will not." [30] And Jesus said to him, "Truly, I say to you, this very night, before the cock crows twice, you will deny me three times." [31] But he said vehemently, "If I must die with you, I will not deny you." And they all said the same.
[32] And they went to a place which was called

Gethse-mane; and he said to his disciples, "Sit here, while I pray." [33] And he took with him Peter and James and John, and began to be greatly distressed and troubled. [34] And he said to them, "My soul is very sorrowful, even to death; remain here, and watch." [35] And going a little farther, he fell on the ground and prayed that, if it were possible, the hour might pass from him. [36] And he said, "Abba, Father, all things are possible to thee; remove this cup from me; yet not what I will, but what thou wilt." [37] And he came and found them sleeping, and he said to Peter, "Simon, are you asleep? Could you not watch one hour? [38] Watch and pray that you may not enter into temptation; the spirit indeed is willing, but the flesh is weak." [39] And again he went away and prayed, saying the same words. [40] And again he came and found them sleeping, for their eyes were very heavy; and they did not know what to answer him. [41] And he came the third time, and said to them, "Are you still sleeping and taking your rest? It is enough; the hour has come; the Son of man is betrayed into the hands of sinners. [42] Rise; let us be going; see, my betrayer is at hand."

[43] And immediately, while he was still speaking, Judas came, one of the twelve, and with him a crowd with swords and clubs, from the chief priests and the scribes and the elders. [44] Now the betrayer had given them a sign, saying, "The one I shall kiss is the man; seize him and lead him away safely." [45] And when he came, he went up to him at once, and said, "Master!" And he kissed him. [46] And they laid hands on him and seized him. [47] But one of those who stood by drew his sword, and struck the slave of the high priest and cut off his ear. [48] And Jesus said to them, "Have you come out as against a robber, with swords and clubs to capture me? [49] Day after day I was with you in the temple teaching, and you did not seize me. But let the scriptures be fulfilled." [50] And they all forsook him, and fled.

⁵¹   And a young man followed him, with nothing but a
linen cloth about his body; and they seized him, ⁵² but he
left the linen cloth and ran away naked.
⁵³   And they led Jesus to the high priest; and all the
chief priests and the elders and the scribes were
assembled. ⁵⁴ And Peter had followed him at a distance,
right into the courtyard of the high priest; and he was
sitting with the guards, and warming himself at the fire.
⁵⁵ Now the chief priests and the whole council sought
testimony against Jesus to put him to death; but they
found none. ⁵⁶ For many bore false witness against him,
and their witness did not agree. ⁵⁷ And some stood up
and bore false witness against him, saying, ⁵⁸ "We heard
him say, 'I will destroy this temple that is made with
hands, and in three days I will build another, not made
with hands.' " ⁵⁹ Yet not even so did their testimony
agree. ⁶⁰And the high priest stood up in the midst, and
asked Jesus, "Have you no answer to make? What is it
that these men testify against you?" ⁶¹ But he was silent
and made no answer. Again the high priest asked him,
"Are you the Christ, the Son of the Blessed?" ⁶² And
Jesus said, "I am; and you will see the Son of man seated
at the right hand of Power, and coming with the clouds
of heaven." ⁶³ And the high priest tore his mantle, and
said, "Why do we still need witnesses? ⁶⁴ You have heard
his blasphemy. What is your decision?" And they all
condemned him as deserving death. ⁶⁵ And some began
to spit on him, and to cover his face, and to strike him,
saying to him, "Prophesy!" And the guards received him
with blows.
⁶⁶   And as Peter was below in the courtyard, one of the
maids of the high priest came; ⁶⁷ and seeing Peter warm-

ing himself, she looked at him, and said, "You also were with the Nazarene, Jesus." [68] But he denied it, saying, "I neither know nor understand what you mean." And he went out into the gateway. [69] And the maid saw him, and began again to say to the bystanders, "This man is one of them." [70] But again he denied it. And after a little while again the bystanders said to Peter, "Certainly you are one of them; for you are a Galilean." [71] But he began to invoke a curse on himself and to swear, "I do not know this man of whom you speak." [72] And immediately the cock crowed a second time. And Peter remembered how Jesus had said to him, "Before the cock crows twice, you will deny me three times." And he broke down and wept.

Mark 15:1-47

[1]   And as soon as it was morning the chief priests, with the elders and scribes, and the whole council held a consultation; and they bound Jesus and led him away and delivered him to Pilate. [2] And Pilate asked him, "Are you the King of the Jews?" And he answered him, "You have said so." [3] And the chief priests accused him of many things. [4] And Pilate again asked him, "Have you no answer to make? See how many charges they bring against you." [5] But Jesus made no further answer, so that Pilate wondered.

[6]   Now at the feast he used to release for them one prisoner whom they asked. [7] And among the rebels in prison, who had committed murder in the insurrection, there was a man called Barabbas. [8] And the crowd came up and began to ask Pilate to do as he was wont to do for them. [9] And he answered them, "Do you want me to release for you the King of the Jews?" [10] For he

perceived that it was out of envy that the chief priests had delivered him up. [11] But the chief priests stirred up the crowd to have him release for them Barabbas instead.

[12] And Pilate again said to them, "Then what shall I do with the man whom you call the King of the Jews?"

[13] And they cried out again, "Crucify him." [14] And Pilate said to them, "Why, what evil has he done?" But they shouted all the more, "Crucify him." [15] So Pilate, wishing to satisfy the crowd, released for them Barabbas; and having scourged Jesus, he delivered him to be crucified.

[16] And the soldiers led him away inside the palace (that is, the praetorium); and they called together the whole battalion. [17] And they clothed him in a purple cloak, and plaiting a crown of thorns they put it on him. [18] And they began to salute him, "Hail, King of the Jews!"

[19] And they struck his head with a reed, and spat upon him, and they knelt down in homage to him. [20] And when they had mocked him, they stripped him of the purple cloak, and put his own clothes on him. And they led him out to crucify him.

[21] And they compelled a passer-by, Simon of Cyrene, who was coming in from the country, the father of Alexander and Rufus, to carry his cross. [22] And they brought him to the place called Golgotha (which means the place of a skull). [23] And they offered him wine mingled with myrrh; but he did not take it. [24] And they crucified him, and divided his garments among them, casting lots for them, to decide what each should take.

[25] And it was the third hour, when they crucified him.

[26] And the inscription of the charge against him read, "The King of the Jews." [27] And with him they crucified two robbers, one on his right and one on his left. [29] And those who passed by derided him, wagging their heads, and saying, "Aha! You who would destroy the temple and build it in three days, [30] save yourself,

and come down from the cross!" [31] So also the chief priests mocked him to one another with the scribes, saying, "He saved others; he cannot save himself. [32] Let the Christ, the King of Israel, come down now from the cross, that we may see and believe." Those who were crucified with him also reviled him. [33] And when the sixth hour had come, there was darkness over the whole land until the ninth hour.

[34] And at the ninth hour Jesus cried with a loud voice, "Elo-i, Elo-i, lama sabach-thani?" which means, "My God, my God, why hast thou forsaken me?" [35] And some of the bystanders hearing it said, "Behold, he is calling Elijah." [36] And one ran and, filling a sponge full of vinegar, put it on a reed and gave it to him to drink, saying, "Wait, let us see whether Elijah will come to take him down." [37] And Jesus uttered a loud cry, and breathed his last. [38] And the curtain of the temple was torn in two, from top to bottom. [39] And when the centurion, who stood facing him, saw that he thus breathed his last, he said, "Truly this man was the Son of God!"

[40] There were also women looking on from afar, among whom were Mary Magdalene, and Mary the mother of James the younger and of Joses, and Salome, [41] who, when he was in Galilee, followed him, and ministered to him; and also many other women who came up with him to Jerusalem.

[42] And when evening had come, since it was the day of Preparation, that is, the day before the sabbath,

[43] Joseph of Arimathea, a respected member of the council, who was also himself looking for the kingdom of God, took courage and went to Pilate, and asked for the body of Jesus. [44] And Pilate wondered if he were already dead; and summoning the centurion, he asked him whether he was already dead. [45] And when he learned from the centurion that he was dead, he granted the body to Joseph. [46] And he bought a linen shroud,

and taking him down, wrapped him in the linen shroud, and laid him in a tomb which had been hewn out of the rock; and he rolled a stone against the door of the tomb.

[47] Mary Magdalene and Mary the mother of Joses saw where he was laid.

Who Do You Say I Am?

The Passion According to Mark

By Gregory Roa

Some commentators of earlier times considered the Gospel of Mark to be the work of "John Mark," the personal secretary of Peter. If so, it would seem rather ironic, for Mark sometimes portrayed Peter in an unflattering light, especially as he recounted Jesus' passion and death narrative. At a time when Jesus needed a friend the most, the chief apostle abandoned him. Twice Peter denied that he was a follower of the Nazarene, and when questioned a third time he replied with his most vehement oath: "I do not know this man" (Mark 14:71).

In one sense, Peter was right! He did not truly know Jesus. He thought he did, but his faith was immature. When Jesus asked his disciples, "Who do you say that I am?" Peter rightly answered, "You are the Christ" (Mark 8:29). It was an important moment of revelation, to be sure. Having witnessed Jesus' many miracles and having heard him teach with authority, Peter voiced the correct answer—but only partially so. Jesus truly was the anointed one of Yahweh, but Peter still needed to understand that Jesus was also the Son of God. The fullness of the revelation of Jesus would come about only in his suffering and death on the Cross, which Jesus immediately pointed to by predicting his passion for the first time (8:31). Peter's attempt to dissuade Jesus from his destiny (8:32-33) made it obvious that he comprehended neither the identity or the mission of the Son of God. His failure would have tragic repercussions during the crisis of the Passion.

Of course, Peter and the other disciples did believe in Jesus, but their vision was impaired, like the blind man whom Jesus had to heal in stages (Mark 8:23-25). By depicting the disciples in this way, Mark invited his original audience, the early church, to identify themselves with the Twelve as they struggled toward deeper understanding. Like this first community of believers, we too are summoned to make the journey to fuller faith. Throughout his gospel, Mark is insistent that only by knowing Jesus in his suffering and death can we know him fully as Messiah and Son of God. This is why Mark shaped his passion narrative as he did—the cross was the key to answering the question that Jesus asks all of his disciples: "Who do you say that I am?"

A Final Moment of Reverence

From the very beginning, Mark portrayed Jesus as a man stalked by death, always pointing us toward the inevitable climax of the cross. As he progressed in his ministry, Jesus faced increasing opposition from the forces of Satan, a conflict that began at the very outset of Jesus' ministry (Mark 1:13). In addition, Jesus was also confronted by the growing enmity of the Jewish religious leaders. From an early point in his public life, they were devising a plan to "destroy him" (3:6). By the time Mark reintroduced the "Pharisees" plot against Jesus—"two days before the Passover" (14:1)—we have been well prepared to understand that this was the culmination of Jesus' entire life and mission.

At the threshold of Jesus' passion, however, Mark paused to tell the story of the woman in Bethany who anointed Jesus with oil. It was a moment of singular tenderness and reverence, and Jesus himself emphasized its significance: "She has anointed my body beforehand for burying. And . . . wherever the gospel is preached in the whole world, what she has done will be told in memory of her" (Mark 14:8-9).

Still, Mark allowed even this wonderful scene of worship to be tinged with irony: Jesus' passion was launched by an act of human kindness performed not by one of his chosen disciples, but by an unnamed woman. As if to underscore the irony, Mark immediately recounted the supreme example of the disciples' failure to understand Jesus: "Then Judas Iscariot, who was one of the twelve, went to the chief priests in order to betray him" (Mark 14:10).

Mark used his sharp sense of irony as a powerful tool. By constantly overturning our expectations and keeping us off guard, Mark invited his readers to look more closely at a familiar story and to allow the Spirit to draw them deeper into the drama of Jesus' passion.

Jesus' Authority: Predictions and a Promise

Though Judas' treachery appeared to place Jesus at the mercy of evil men, Mark was quick to show that Jesus actually retained full control over everything around him. First, Jesus sent "two of his disciples" (Mark 14:13) into the city to prepare the Passover. During their trip, every detail went exactly "as he had told them" (14:16). Then, during the Passover meal, it was Jesus himself who revealed Judas' betrayal (14:18). After the supper, he told them: "You will all fall away" (14:27), and he foretold Peter's three denials (14:30). Clearly, Jesus knew that he would die, and he purposefully allowed it to happen. Even as the cosmic forces of darkness descended upon him, he maintained his authority.

Jesus made one other prediction that evening, not about his disciples but about himself. During the Last Supper, just after he proclaimed the bread and the wine to be his body and blood (Mark 14:22,24), Jesus said, "Truly, I say to you, I shall not drink again of the fruit of the vine until that day when I drink it new in the kingdom of God" (14:25). This solemn vow pointed simultaneously to Jesus' death—"I shall not drink again"— *and* to his victorious resurrection—"until that day I drink it new." Such a twofold statement echoed Jesus' first words recorded in Mark's Gospel, "The time is fulfilled, and the *kingdom of God* is at hand" (1:15). Jesus was about to accomplish his mission on the cross with the breaking of his body and the shedding of the "blood of the covenant." Yet he was already looking beyond the cross to the wondrous new age that his sacrifice was about to usher in. Linked as they are to the sacramental formula of the liturgy, Jesus' promise can be taken as a sign for all who share communion with him. On that night, he made a personal pledge to all of us: "Unite yourself to my body, share in the cup of my suffering, and we will sup together in my Father's kingdom." Such a promise must have been particularly meaningful for Mark's original readers who daily faced the threat of death and persecution.

Suffering Messiah and Son of God

Aware of the hardships that the early Christian community faced, Mark made it abundantly clear that the Jesus whom they worshipped had experienced a suffering as intense as their own. In the Garden of Gethsemane, Jesus became "greatly distressed and troubled" (Mark 14:33) and said: "My soul is very sorrowful, even to death" (14:34). Mark then showed the depth of Jesus' anguish by repeating his prayer in this desperate hour: "Abba, Father, all things are possible to you; remove this cup from me; yet not what I will, but what you will" (14:36). Of the synoptic writers, only Mark retained the Aramaic word "Abba," the diminutive and affectionate form of addressing one's father, best translated as "daddy." Somehow, the word "Abba" makes Jesus seem all the more vulnerable, a person who shares in all of our weaknesses and fears. Yet, at the same time, Jesus' human cry for help identified his true origin—he is able to address the Almighty God as "Abba." The Son was doing exactly what his Father had asked of him—"to give his life as a ransom for many" (10:45). Having accepted the Father's will, he declared: "Let the scriptures be fulfilled" (14:49), and he was handed over to be tried and executed.

Here is the central paradox of Mark's Gospel: While Jesus was performing miracles and exorcising demons—the time when he appeared most divine—he refused to be called anything but the Son of man. He hid his divine nature from the world—it was his "Messianic secret." Yet now, having reached the place of full disclosure, Jesus began at last to assume the titles of divinity that were rightfully his all along. Ironically, it was here at the place of revelation that Jesus appeared the most mortal, lonely, and forsaken. Even his closest friends "all forsook him and fled" (Mark 14:50). When he appeared most truly to be a mortal "Son of man," Mark lifted the veil and showed him to be the Son of God.

The tables are now turned. Jesus was no longer asking: "Who do you say that I am?" In a reversal of roles, Jesus was now being asked the question: "Who do *you* say *you* are?" The high priest pressed Jesus for an answer: "Are you the Christ, the Son of the Blessed?" (Mark 14:61). Jesus confessed: "I am" (14:62), not merely affirming that he is the Messiah but amplifying it with an unmistakable allusion to God's sacred name (see Exodus 3:14). He continued: "And you will see the Son of man sitting at the right hand of Power, and coming with the clouds of heaven" (14:62). By echoing Jesus' own apocalyptic imagery of "coming in clouds with great power" (13:26), Mark emphasized that Jesus' death ushered in the end of this world and the start of the kingdom of God. The allusion similarly comforted the early Christians by reminding them that even though sorrow and pain will accompany the birth of the new age, those who suffer with Christ will reign with him when he is revealed in glory.

Pilate offered Jesus yet another title by asking: "Are you the King of the Jews?" (Mark 15:2). Though the question was politically charged, Jesus nonetheless accepted it. Then, in a cruel parody of a royal coronation ceremony, the Roman soldiers clothed and crowned Jesus (15:17), then paraded him before his "subjects"—the people of Israel. They gladly joined in the derision by supplying him with yet another divine title—"the King of Israel"

(15:32). With somber irony, the Romans and the Jews, who had been bitter enemies, were now united in the crucifixion of Jesus, little realizing that they were the ones who had uncovered the truth about Jesus (15:26).

Mark's Passion narrative begins with an anonymous woman anointing Jesus, calling to mind his title, "Christ"—the "Anointed One." Now, as the struggle ended, Mark introduced a second stranger bearing witness to the truth about Jesus. "Jesus uttered a loud cry, and breathed his last. . . . And when the centurion, who stood facing him, saw that he thus breathed his last, he said, 'Truly this man was the Son of God!' " (Mark 15:37-39). Neither a disciple or a Jew, this Roman soldier discovered in the death of Jesus the long-sought answer to the question: "Who do you say that I am?" With these two ironic figures Mark framed the revelation within the Passion narrative and simultaneously brought his entire account full circle by affirming that it is truly "the gospel of Jesus Christ, the Son of God" (1:1).

The Wisdom of the Cross

In Mark's ironic construct, Jesus' moment of triumph was also the moment of his death. At what seemed to be the darkest hour, after everything has completely fallen apart and the miracle-worker lay dead at the hands of his enemies, a human voice at last echoes the heavenly Father's words: "You are my beloved Son" (Mark 1:11). The cross fulfilled the ministry of the Son of man who came "to give his life as a ransom for many" (10:45).

As he recounted the story of the cross, Mark sought to teach his readers that discipleship begins at the cross. Like the women who stood with Jesus during the crucifixion, we are called to follow him, and minister to him (Mark 15:41). Significantly, the two women Mark identifies are the same pair that first heard of Jesus' resurrection (16:1). While the unbeliever demanded, "Let the Christ . . . come down now from the cross, that we may see and believe" (15:32), the person of faith joined the "women looking on from afar" (15:40). Those who see in Jesus' Passion his victory over death are able to take "courage" like Joseph of Arimathea (15:43). They become true disciples of Jesus Christ, the suffering Son of man who declared, "If any man would come after me, let him deny himself and take up his cross and follow me" (8:34).

Mark wrote his narrative for a young church beleaguered by persecution, but his message remains a word of encouragement and challenge to us today. Will we let our faith be blunted by failure, loneliness, and setbacks? Or will we, like Jesus, place our trust in our "Abba" in heaven? Will we see with disciples' eyes the revelation of God who is with us even amid the chaos of our struggle against sin and death? Mark's narrative discloses the wonderful truth concisely summarized in the *Catechism of the Catholic Church*:

By his passion and death on the cross Christ has given a new meaning to suffering: it can henceforth configure us to him and unite us with his redemptive Passion. (1505)

A Devotional Commentary on Mark

The Empty Tomb and the Resurrection

MARK
16

Mark 16:1-8

[1] And when the sabbath was past, Mary Magdalene, and Mary the mother of James, and Salome, bought spices, so that they might go and anoint him. [2] And very early on the first day of the week they went to the tomb when the sun had risen. [3] And they were saying to one another, "Who will roll away the stone for us from the door of the tomb?" [4] And looking up, they saw that the stone was rolled back; for it was very large. [5] And entering the tomb, they saw a young man sitting on the right side, dressed in a white robe; and they were amazed. [6] And he said to them, "Do not be amazed; you seek Jesus of Nazareth, who was crucified. He has risen, he is not here; see the place where they laid him. [7] But go, tell his disciples and Peter that he is going before you to Galilee; there you will see him, as he told you." [8] And they went out and fled from the tomb; for trembling and astonishment had come upon them; and they said nothing to any one, for they were afraid.

From an Easter homily by St. Melito of Sardis:

For the sake of suffering humanity, Christ came down from heaven to earth, clothed himself in that humanity in the Virgin's womb, and was born a man. Having a body capable of suffering, he took the pain of fallen man upon himself; he triumphed over the diseases of soul and body that were its cause, and by his Spirit . . . he dealt man's destroyer, death, a fatal blow.

He was led forth like a lamb; he was slaughtered like a sheep. He ransomed us from our servitude to the world, as he had ransomed

Israel from the land of Egypt; he freed us from our slavery to the devil, as he had freed Israel from the hand of Pharaoh. He sealed our souls with his own Spirit, and the members of our body with his own blood.

He is the One who covered death with shame and cast the devil into mourning, as Moses cast Pharaoh into mourning. He is the One who smote sin and robbed iniquity of offspring, as Moses robbed the Egyptians of their offspring. He is the One who brought us out of slavery into freedom, out of darkness into light, out of death into life, out of tryanny into an eternal kingdom; who made us a new priesthood, a people chosen to be his own forever.

In Abel he was slain, in Isaac bound, in Jacob exiled, in Joseph sold, in Moses exposed to die. He was sacrificed in the Passover lamb, persecuted in David, dishonored in the prophets.

It is he who was made man of the Virgin, he who was hung on the tree; it is he who was buried in the earth, raised from the dead and taken up to the heights of heaven. . . . On the tree no bone of his was broken; in the earth his body knew no decay. He is the One who rose from the dead, and who raised the human race from the depths of the tomb.

Mark 16:9-15

[9] Now when he rose early on the first day of the week, he appeared first to Mary Magdalene, from whom he had cast out seven demons. [10] She went and told those who had been with him, as they mourned and wept. [11] But when they heard that he was alive and had been seen by her, they would not believe it. [12] After this he appeared in another form to two of them, as they were walking into the country. [13] And they went back and told the rest, but they did not believe them. [14] Afterward he appeared to the eleven themselves as they sat at table; and he upbraided them for their unbelief and hardness of heart, because they had not believed those who saw him after he had risen. [15] And he said to them, "Go into all the world and preach the gospel to the whole creation."

Go into all the world and preach the gospel to the whole creation.
(Mark 16:15)

This command given by Jesus to his disciples is similar to God's command to Adam and Eve when he blessed them and said, "Be fruitful and multiply, and fill the earth and subdue it" (Genesis 1:28).

The commands were similar, but those who received them were in quite different circumstances. The command of Jesus is given to a people living after the time of the transforming event of Jesus' death and resurrection. It is a word for those who have listened to Jesus, believed in him, and are being transformed by grace. Jesus' direction is meant for those who have been lifted up to new life and are empowered by the Holy Spirit.

Made capable of obeying God by the power of the Spirit, they go forth with the authority of the Father, Son, and Holy Spirit to bear good fruit for God. Their going forth brings great joy to God: "By this my Father is glorified, that you bear much fruit and so prove to be my disciples" (John 15:8).

Our own inner commitment to Christ must be at the core of our proclamation of the gospel. Pope John Paul II told the bishops of Lombardy in 1992: "For the new evangelization it is necessary to pass from faith based on traditions—even good ones—to a personal, enlightened, convicted witness." Without this inner conviction, our efforts to evangelize and proclaim the gospel often lack power and credibility. We tend to rely on remembered facts instead of lived experience; we easily grow weary; timidity sometimes constrains us.

The new creation, on the other hand, because he or she knows the love of Jesus and the seed of faith planted at baptism is growing, makes a credible witness. This person knows that the promises of God are true and lives in a way that bears witness to them. Such a man or woman is sustained by God, each day striving to be in communion with him.

"Lord Jesus, we have received your call to go into all the world and proclaim the good news. Make me a spark of light, a center of love, a vivifying leaven in the world and give me the courage to speak your word of truth in love."

Mark 16:16-20

¹⁶ [Jesus said,] "He who believes and is baptized will be saved; but he who does not believe will be condemned. ¹⁷And these signs will accompany those who believe: in my name they will cast out demons; they will speak in new tongues; ¹⁸ they will pick up serpents, and if they drink any deadly thing, it will not hurt them; they will lay their hands on the sick, and they will recover."
¹⁹ So then the Lord Jesus, after he had spoken to them, was taken up into heaven, and sat down at the right hand of God. ²⁰ And they went forth and preached everywhere, while the Lord worked with them and confirmed the message by the signs that attended it. Amen.

This passage from the Gospel of Mark is part of the canonical ending and is accepted as the inspired word of God even though it was not written by Mark himself. In it, the Lord instructs his followers, saying, "Go into all the world and preach the gospel to the whole creation. He who believes and is baptized will be saved; but he who does not believe will be condemned" (Mark 16:15-16). The preaching of the good news brings either life or death to every person based on a response of belief or unbelief.

We also find here the promise of the power that will accompany this preaching of the gospel. Jesus has won eternal salvation for all who will believe in him. By his death and resurrection, he has conquered every power that would stand against him. Because of the authority in the name of Jesus, we also will experience deliverance, healing, and power as we stand by Christ. When we share with our families and friends about what Jesus has done in our lives, we can withstand and overcome unbelief, ignorance, and fear. The result will be life and healing to those with whom we come into contact.

The source of our power is rooted in our humble trust in God: "God opposes the proud, but gives grace to the humble" (1 Peter 5:5). Only as we know personally that we have been saved from certain death because of our sins will we have the confidence to call upon God and ask for his grace and wisdom. When we remember our deliverance each day, we will come to know with certainty the love and care of God.

After Jesus had spoken to his disciples, he was taken up to heaven where he now reigns in majesty. The disciples went forth, as we are called to go forth. Let us turn to the heavens for the grace and strength promised to all who desire to do the will of God.

"Lord Jesus, etch into our hearts and minds the knowledge of your saving action in our lives. Empower us, through your Holy Spirit, to preach this good news to all of those you put in our path."

Topical Index of Mark's Gospel

Events in the Life of Jesus:

Healings:

Other Resources From The Word Among Us Press

Also from the Gospel Devotional Commentary Series:
Matthew: A Devotional Commentary
Luke: A Devotional Commentary
John: A Devotional Commentary
Leo Zanchettin, General Editor

Enjoy reading and praying through the gospels with commentaries that include each passage of scripture with a faith-filled meditation.

Books on the Saints:
A Great Cloud of Witnesses—The Stories of 16 Saints and Christian Heroes by Leo Zanchettin and Patricia Mitchell

I Have Called You by Name—The Stories of 16 Saints and Christian Heroes by Patricia Mitchell

Each book contains practical, down-to-earth biographies along with selections of the saints' own writings and time lines to provide historical context.

The Wisdom Series:
The writings from these spiritual masters become more accessible to the contemporary reader in The Word Among Us Wisdom series. These popular books include short biographies of the authors and selections from their writings grouped around themes such as prayer, forgiveness, and mercy.

Welcoming the New Millennium, Wisdom from Pope John Paul II

My Heart Speaks, Wisdom from Pope John XXIII

Live Jesus! Wisdom from Saints Francis de Sales and Jane de Chantal

A Radical Love, Wisdom from Dorothy Day

Love Songs, Wisdom from St. Bernard of Clairvaux

Walking with the Father, Wisdom from Brother Lawrence

Touching the Risen Christ, Wisdom from the Fathers

To order call 1-800-775-9673 or order online at www.wau.org